Henrietta Dumont

The lady's oracle

an elegant pastime for social parties and the family circle

Henrietta Dumont

The lady's oracle
an elegant pastime for social parties and the family circle

ISBN/EAN: 9783337374198

Printed in Europe, USA, Canada, Australia, Japan

Cover: Foto ©Andreas Hilbeck / pixelio.de

More available books at **www.hansebooks.com**

THE

LADY'S ORACLE:

AN ELEGANT PASTIME

FOR

𝔖𝔬𝔠𝔦𝔞𝔩 𝔓𝔞𝔯𝔱𝔦𝔢𝔰 𝔞𝔫𝔡 𝔱𝔥𝔢 𝔉𝔞𝔪𝔦𝔩𝔶 𝔆𝔦𝔯𝔠𝔩𝔢.

By HENRIETTA DUMONT.

PHILADELPHIA:
H. C. PECK & THEO. BLISS.
1860.

A 458915

STEREOTYPED BY L. JOHNSON AND CO.
PHILADELPHIA.

Preface.

WHEN a social party of young people is assembled for an evening's enjoyment, it sometimes happens that conversation flags, and every one feels the necessity of some movement which shall dissipate the awkwardness and restraint of the moment, and afford the means of active and interesting amusement. Some elegant pastime, which affords an opportunity for the flow of remark and the play of fancy, then becomes a desideratum; and it is precisely to supply this desideratum, that the following volume has been compiled. It is a game of questions and answers between a lady and gentleman; and may be carried successively round a whole circle, all giving attention to each question and each answer.

The answers being quoted from standard poets, and made by a chance choice of numbers, all appearance of personality is avoided, and the amusement,

which often occasions the liveliest mirth, is free
from every ground of offence.

Some of the answers are of a highly humorous
character, while others are grave, sentimental, or
patriotic. As there is a large number of questions,
and fifty answers to each question, a company will
find sufficient entertainment in it to last a whole
evening, and for many evenings in succession. In
fact, the possession of such a book in a family will
afford the means of entertainment to a party of
friends, whenever books, prints, music, dancing, and
the ordinary games of social parties fail.

The good effects of an amusement of the intellec-
tual kind which we propose, are manifold. The
frequent repetition of choice extracts from standard
poets, stores the mind with agreeable images, im-
proves the taste, and familiarizes the ear to the
musical rhythm of good poetry; it also enlarges the
vocabulary, and increases the conversational powers.
But the chief value of the game is still the present
advantage derived from the pleasure it affords in
playing it.

We hold to the doctrine that one renders a real
bonâ fide benefit to mankind, who proposes a new
innocent amusement. In our country particularly,

we work too hard, and we think too much and too
anxiously about business, and money, and household
cares, and our future worldly prosperity; the con-
sequence is, that we wear out our minds and bodies
too soon. If we gave more time to innocent recrea-
tion, we should enjoy better health, live longer,
and perform more service to our friends, our
families, and our country. When the day's work,
a fair day's work is done, it is our duty to relax our
minds from all worldly care, trust the morrow to
Providence, and give the evening to our friends and
to innocent recreation. By so doing, we increase
the sum of human happiness without violating any
law, human or divine.

We are aware that many of our readers will re-
gard these as self-evident truths, which it is hardly
worth while to repeat; but we know very well that
there are others who are so earnestly engaged in the
pursuit of worldly wealth and honour, that they
esteem every hour spent in amusement of any kind
as a dead loss. This is a grave error, especially in
a young person; and those who entertain such
views should recollect that an exclusive devotion to
worldly advancement is wrong; it distorts the cha-
racter; it renders sorrow and chastisement neces-

sary, in order to soften and humanize the disposition, and prepare the soul for that world where the greatest worldly advancement is of no value whatever.

List of Questions.

11

Directions for Consulting the Oracle.

The person who holds the book asks the question. The person whose fortune is to be read selects any one of the fifty answers under that question, say No. 10, and the questioner reads aloud the answer No. 10, which will be the Oracle.

𝔚𝔥𝔞𝔱 𝔞𝔯𝔢 𝔶𝔬𝔲𝔯 𝔰𝔢𝔫𝔱𝔦𝔪𝔢𝔫𝔱𝔰 𝔱𝔬𝔴𝔞𝔯𝔡𝔰 𝔪𝔢?

Gentleman.

*I like you not; you laugh when
And mope when I am merry*

MY

Ramsay.

2. I am no pilot; yet wert thou as far
   As that vast shore washed with the farthest sea,
   I would adventure for such merchandise.
                              Shakspeare.

3. Get thee to a nunnery!
                              Shakspeare.

4.   Never yet did mariner
   Put up to patron saint such prayers for prosperous
   And pleasant breezes as I call upon you.
                              Byron.

13

5. There is a fair behaviour in thee.
   And though that nature with a beauteous wall
   Doth oft close in pollution, yet of thee
   I will believe thou hast a mind that suits
   With this thy fair and outward character.

   Shakspeare.

6. Thou livest in my heart, through distance—time,
   Midst fickle friendships and fantastic joys,
   Alone a truth:—like Love, which is sublime,
   Thy sweet smile elevates, and never cloys.

   Barry Cornwall.

7. Bonnie Mary Hay, I will lo'e thee yet;
   For thy eye is the slae, and thy hair is the jet,
   The snaw is thy skin, and the rose is thy cheek:
   Oh! bonnie Mary Hay, I will lo'e thee yet.

   Crawford.

8. But if fond love thy heart can gain,
   I never broke a vow;
   Nae maiden lays her skaith to me;
   I never loved but you.

   Graham.

9. Oh, sweet grow the lime and the orange,
   And the apple on the pine;
   But a' the charms o' the Indies
   Can never equal thine.

   Burns.

10. I'll have thy beauty scratched with briers,
And made more homely than thy state.

Shakspeare.

11. A little word in kindness spoken,
A motion or a tear,
Has often healed the heart that's broken,
And made a friend sincere.

Bridell.

12. Affection is lowly and deep;
All groundless suspicion above,
It knows but to trust or to weep.

Mrs. Ellis.

13. How divinely sweet
Is the pure joy when kindred spirits meet.

Moore.

14. Like as the ivy round the elm doth wreathe,
So friendship twines, nor quits its hold till death.

Friend.

15. As fair art thou, my bonnie lass,
Sae deep in love am I;
And I will love thee still, my dear,
Till a' the seas gang dry.

Burns.

16. A gaudy dress and gentle air
May slightly touch the heart,
But it's innocence and modesty
That polishes the dart.

Burns.

17. O how much more doth beauty beauteous seem
   By that sweet ornament which truth doth give;
The rose looks fair, but fairer we it deem
 For that sweet odour which doth in it live.
Shakspeare.

18. There's nane to me wi' her can vie,
   I'll love her till I dee,
For she's sae sweet, and bonnie, aye,
   And kind as kind can be.
Cameron.

19. The tender glance, the reddening cheek,
   O'erspread with rising blushes,
A thousand various ways they speak
   A thousand various wishes.
Hamilton.

20. What I most prize in woman
Is her affections, not her intellect!
The intellect is finite, but the affections
Are infinite, and cannot be exhausted.
Compare me with the great men of the earth:
What am I? Why, a pigmy among giants!
But if thou lovest—mark me! I say lovest!
The greatest of thy sex excels thee not!
Longfellow

21. Oh, woman, oft misconstrued! the pure pearls
Lie all too deep in thy heart's secret well,
For the unpausing and impatient hand
To win them forth.
Sigourney.

22. My soul is ravished with delight
    When you I think upon;
  All griefs and sorrows take their flight,
    And hastily are gone:
  The fair resemblance of your face
    So fills this breast of mine,
  No fate nor force can it displace,
    For old long syne.
                        Old Song.

23. Oh, how can beautie master the most strong!
                        Spenser.

24. I've wandered east, I've wandered west,
    I've borne a weary lot;
  But in my wanderings, far or near,
    Ye never were forgot.
                        Motherwell.

25. May health, life's greatest blessing,
    Beam on thy cheek and brow;
  Be thine love's fond caressing
    Wi' ane whase heart is true.
                        Charles Gray.

26. O come to my arms, lassie, charming an' fair,
    Awa' wild alarms, lassie dear;
  This fond heart an' thine like ivy shall twine,
    I'll lo'e thee, dear, till the day that I dee.
                        Jaap.

2

27. Nocht's to be gained at woman's hand,
    Unless ye gi'e her a' the plea;
  Then I'll leave aff where I began,
    And tak' my auld cloak about me.
                          Ramsay.

28. But though thy fair and faithless air
    Hath wrung the bosom-sigh frae me;
  A changing mind and heart unkind
    May chill a breast as dear to thee
                          Ivan.

29. Witless hizzie, e'ens ye like,
    The ne'er a doit I'm carin';
  But men maun be the first to speak,
    An' wanters maun be speirin'.
                          A. L.

30. I prize your smile as husbandman
    The summer's opening bloom;
  And, could you frown, I dread it mair
    Than he the autumn's gloom.
                          Ferguson.

31. To see thee in anither's arms,
    In love to lie and languish,
  'Twad be my dead, that will be seen,
    My heart wad burst wi' anguish.
                          Burns.

32. Ye're my ain, love, ye're my ain!
    Forms sae fair, I ne'er see mony;
  Hearts sae fond, sae true, love, nane!
    Ye're my ain! my dear! my bonny!
                          Knowles.

33. Fondly wooing, fondly sueing,
    Let me love, nor love in vain;
    Fate shall never fond hearts sever,
    Hearts still bound by true love's chain.
                         Allan.

34. Lassie, I maun leave you too,
    Though I lo'e you best o' ony;
    Ye ha'e wooers mony ane,
    Ye winna ken the want o' Johnny!
                         Laing.

35. A boon may I venture to beg frae thee, Heaven?
    Amid a' my care, an' my toil, an' my fear,
    Be the heart-warmin' impulse o' frien'ship me given.
    To live in her smile, or be worthy her tear.
                         Scotch Song.

36. Go fetch to me a pint o' wine,
    And fill it in a silver tassie;
    That I may drink before I go,
    A service to my bonnie lassie.
                         Burns.

37. For while I gaze my bosom glows,
    My blood in tides impetuous flows;
    Hope, fear, and joy, alternate roll,
    And floods of transport 'whelm my soul.
                         Smollett.

38. There's nane can tell what's yet to come,
    But round my heart I will entwine
    The hope that time will bring the day
    When I can ca' yon lassie mine.
                         Steele.

39. When I see you, I love you; when hearing, adore;
    I wonder, and think you a woman no more;
    Till, mad wi' admiring, I canna contain,
    And, kissing your lips, you turn woman again.
                                            Webster.

40. A bonnie lass, I will confess,
        Is pleasant to the e'e,
    But without some better qualities,
        She's no a lass for me.

                                            Burns.

41. Ah! could you look into my heart,
        And watch your image there,
    You would own the sunny loveliness
        Affection makes it wear.
                                            Mrs. Osgood.

42. Oh! no, my heart can never be
        Again in lightest hopes the same;
    The love that lingers there for thee
        Hath more of ashes than of flame!
                                            Miss Landon.

43. Your life is like the living sun,
        That gi'es life to the plain;
    Though clouds awhile may dim his smile,
        He'll brighter beam again.
    I wouldna be the cloud that comes
        Atween your love an' ye;
    Your life's sweet light—the light o' lo'e,
        Lo'e glentin' frae the e'e.
                                            Bennoch.

44. Bonnie wee thing, cannie wee thing,
    Lovely wee thing, wert thou mine,
I wad wear thee in my bosom,
    Lest my jewel I should tine.
                         Burns.

45. How sweet to view that face so meek,
    That dark expressive eye;
To kiss that lovely blushing cheek,
    Those lips of coral dye.
                         Rodger,

46. Dear child, how could I wrong thy name?
    Thy form so fair and faultless stands,
That could ill tongues abuse thy fame,
    Thy beauty would make large amends!
                         Hamilton.

47. Thy voice trembles through me
    Like the breeze,
That ruffles, in gladness,
    The leafy trees;
'Tis a wafted tone
From heaven's high throne,
Making hearts thine own,
    My Mary dhu.
                         Moir.

48. And yet I love thee with a love
    That cannot fade or pass away;
And time alone such love can prove,
    As orient sunshine proves the day.
                         Nevay.

49. Must Robin always Nannie woo?
    And Nannie still on Robin frown?
Alas, poor wretch! what shall I do,
    If Nannie does not love me soon?
If no relief to me she'll bring,
I'll hang me in her apron string.

                    Hamilton.

50. I'm jealous o' what blesses her,
The very breeze that kisses her,
    The flowery beds
    On which she treads,
Though wae for ane that misses her.

                    James Hogg.

What are your sentiments towards me?

Lady.

WHISTLE, and I'll come to you, my lad;
  O, whistle, and I'll come to you, my lad;
  Tho' father, and mother, and a' should gae mad,
  O, whistle and I'll come to you, my lad.

Bruce.

2. O, Sandy is a braw lad,
     An' Sandy is a fine,
   An' Sandy is a bonnie lad,
     An' best of a', he's mine!

Hetherington.

3. Gae, get you gone, you cauldrife wooer,
   Ye sour-looking, cauldrife wooer!

Herd.

4. I ha'e a wooer o' my ain,
     They ca' him souple Sandy,
   And weel I wat his bonnie mou'
     Is sweet like sugar-candy.

Old Scotch Song.

23

5. For all the gold and all the gear,
   And all the lands, both far and near,
   That ever valour lost or won,
   I will not wed the Earlie's son.

W. Scott.

6. Amazed was the laird when the lady said, Na,
   And wi' a laigh curtsie she turned awa'.

Miss Ferrier.

7. I read thy letters sent from far,
   And aft I kiss thy name,
   And ask my Maker, frae the war
   If ever thou'lt come hame, Willie.

Wilson.

8. Sae lieht's he jumped up the stair,
   And tirled at the pin;
   And wha sae ready as hersel'
   To let the laddie in!

Old Jacobite Song.

9. For the sake of somebody,
   For the sake of somebody,
   I could wake a winter nicht,
   For the sake of somebody.

Ramsay.

10. But blythely will I bide
   Whate'er may yet betide,
   When ane is by my side.

Smibert.

11. Maggie cuist her head fu' heich,
Looked asklant, and unco skeigh,
While puir Duncan stood abeigh—
Ha, ha, the wooing o't.
Burns.

12. But old Rob Morris I never will ha'e,
His back is so stiff, and his beard is grown gray;
I had rather die than live wi' him a year;
Sae mair o' Rob Morris I never will hear.
Ramsay.

13. The maiden blushed and bing'd fu' law,
She hadna will to say him na,
But to her daddy she left it a',
As they twa cou'd agree.
Ramsay.

14. My minnie does constantly warn me,
And bids me beware o' young men;
They flatter, she says, to deceive me—
But wha can think sae o' Tam Glen?
Burns.

15. Hout awa'! I winna ha'e him!
Na, forsooth, I winna ha'e him!
For a' his beard new-shaven,
Ne'er a bit o' me will ha'e him.
Ramsay.

16. When day, expiring in the west,
The curtain draws o' Nature's rest,
I'll flee to his arms I lo'e best,
And that's my dainty Davie.
Burns.

17. And though ye vowed ye wad be mine,
    The tear o' grief aye dims my e'e,
For, O! I'm feared that I may tyne
    The love that ye ha'e promis'd me!
Tannahill.

18. My father has baith gowd and gear,
    Forby a bonnie mailen free:
My mither spins wi' eident care,
    An' dochtors they ha'e nane but me.
 But what care I for gowd and gear,
    Or what care I for mailens free?
I wadna gi'e a bonnie lad
    For a' the gowd in Chrisendie.
W. Paul.

19. O come, my love, the branches link
    Above our bed of blossoms new,
The stars behind their curtains wink,
    To spare thine eyes so soft and blue.
No human eye nor heavenly gem,
    With envious smile, our bliss shall see;
The mountain ash his diadem
    Shall spread to shield the dews from thee.
James Hogg

20. O, how can I be blithe and glad,
    Or how can I gang brisk and braw,
When the bonnie lad that I lo'e best
    Is o'er the hills and far awa'?
Burns

21. His words sae sweet gaed to my heart,
And fain I wad ha'e gi'en my han'.
Hamilton.

22. Were I young for thee, as I ha'e been,
We should ha'e been gallopin' down on yon green,
And linkin' it on yon lilie-white lea;
And wow! gin I were but young for thee!
Home.

23. He's on tho seas to meet his foe!
. Let me wander, let me rove,
Still my heart is with my love;
Nightly dreams and thoughts by day
Are with him that's far away.
Burns.

24. My head is like to rend, Willie,
My heart is like to break—
I'm wearin' aff my feet, Willie,
I'm dyin' for your sake!
Motherwell.

25. But, gin you really do insist
That I should suffer to be kiss'd,
Gae, get a license frae the priest,
And mak' me yours before folk.
Rodger.

26. Ye've heard o' my tocher in gear an' good brass,
An' ye ken that ilk pound gi'es a charm to a lass;
But if pounds be my beauties, your love's unco
chill;
Lad! I'll awa' hame to my mither, I will.
Rodger.

27. I've lo'ed thee o'er truly to seek a new dearie,
    I've lo'ed thee o'er fondly, through life e'er to weary,
    I've lo'ed thee o'er lang, love, at last to deceive thee:
    Look cauldly or kindly, but bid me not leave thee."
                                        Macgregor.

28. Never wedding, ever wooing,
    Still a love-torn heart pursuing;
    Read you not the wrongs you're doing,
      In my cheek's pale hue?
    All my life with sorrow strewing,
      Wed—or cease to woo.
                                        Campbell.

29.   Love is timid, Love is shy,
         Can you tell me, tell me why?
      Ah! tell me, why true love should be
         Afraid to meet the kindly smile
      Of him she loves, from him would flee,
         Yet thinks upon him all the while?
                                        Weir.

30. Somebody's words are wonderfu' words,
      They're wonderfu' words to hear;
    Somebody's words can lighten the heart,
      Or fill the e'e wi' a tear.
    They may say's they like, they may do's they like,
      An' somebody I may tine;
    But I'll live's I am, an' I'll die's I am,
      If somebody mayna be mine.
                                        Gibson.

31. Young Donald is the blithest lad
    That e'er made love to me;
    Whene'er he's by my heart is glad,
    He seems so gay and free.

Anon.

32. Tam I esteem, like him there's few,
    His gait and looks entice me.

Lochore.

33. Thou canst love another jo,
    While my heart is breaking:
    Soon my weary e'en I'll close,
    Never more to waken, Jamie.

Burns.

34. Never, Henry, could I leave thee,
    Never could this heart deceive thee;
    Why then, laddie, me forsake,
    And sae wi' cruel absence grieve me?

Stirrat.

35. I swear and vow that only thou
    Shall ever be my dearie.
    Only thou, I swear and vow,
    Shall ever be my dearie.

Burns.

36. She said, If that your heart be true,
    If constantly you'll love me,
    I heed not care nor fortune's frowns,
    For naught but death shall move me.

Tytler.

Missing Page

Missing Page

49. A slight blush, a soft tremor, a calm kind
    Of gentle feminine delight, and shown
More in the eyelids than the eyes, resigned
    Rather to his what pleases, most unknown,
Are the best tokens to a modest mind
    Of Love, when seated on his loveliest throne,
A sincere woman's heart.

Byron.

50. The shaken tree grows faster at the root;
    And Love grows firmer for some blasts of doubt.
Carcanet.

Describe the Personal Appearance of your Lady-love.

Answered by a Gentleman.

HER yellow hair, beyond compare,
    Comes trinkling down her swan-white neck;
    And her two eyes, like stars in skies,
    Would keep a sinking ship frae wreck.
                       Burns.

2. Her poutin' lips sae rosy red
    'Mong laughin' dimples dwell;
  Nae journey-work were they, I trow,
    But made by love himsel'.
Her voice was like a linty's sang,
    Her een were bonnie blue,
And mine drank in the livin' light
    That sparkled through the dew.
                       Latto.

3. She is a winsome wee thing,
  She is a handsome wee thing,
  She is a bonnie wee thing,
    This sweet wee wife o' mine.
                       Burns.

3

4. Her neck was o' the snaw-drap hue,
   Her lips like roses wet wi' dew:
   But oh! her e'e, o' azure blue,
      Was past expressin' bonnie, O.

                                    Nicholson.

5. A fairer face I may have seen,
      And passed it lightly by;
   Louisa's in her tartan sheen
      Has fixed my wandering eye.

                                    Charles Gray.

6. When teddin' out the hay,
      Bareheaded on the green,
   Love mid her locks did play,
      And wantoned in her een.

                                    Ramsay.

7. Her eyes divine more bright did shine
      Than the most clear unclouded ether;
   A fairer form did ne'er adorn
      A brighter scene than blooming heather.

                                    Lewis.

8. Her brow was like a lily flower,
   Smiling 'neath a balmy bower,
   An' glistening i' the mornin' hour
      Amang the dew o' May.
   Her e'e was like the bonnie bell,
   That dances on a sparklin' well,
   When daylight fa's o'er muir an' fell,
      An' wakes the well to play.

                                    Macdonald.

" When teddin' out the hay."

Lady's Oracle, p. 34

9. Oh Nancy's hair is yellow like gowd,
　　An' her een, like the lift, are blue;
　　Her face is the image o' heavenly love,
　　An' her heart is leal and true.
                              Old Scotch Song.

10. I saw, while gazing on her face,
　　　The rose and lily close allied;
　　　And on each bloomin' cheek could trace
　　　The scented apple's sunny side.
　　　Her lips were like the red-rose bud,
　　　　Before the sun has sipped its dew;
　　　Her bosom like the snawy cloud
　　　Reflected in the loch sae blue.
                              Carmichael.

11. Ah no! her form's too heavenly fair,
　　　Her love the gods above must share;
　　　While mortals with despair explore her,
　　　And at distance due adore her.
                              Ramsay.

12. Her look was like the morning's eye,
　　　Her air like nature's vernal smile;
　　　Perfection whispered, passing by,
　　　Behold the lass o' Ballochmyle!
                              Alexander.

13. Grace was in all her steps, heaven in her eye,
　　　In every gesture dignity and love.
                              Milton's Paradise Lost.

14. Oh! sho has beauty might ensnare
    A conqueror's soul, and make him tear his crown
    At random, to be scuffled for by slaves.
                              Otway's Orphan.

15. Yet graceful ease, and sweetness void of pride,
    Might hide her faults, if belles had faults to hide;
    If to her share some female errors fall,
    Look on her face and you'll forget 'em all.
                              Pope's Rape of the Lock.

16. What tender force, what dignity divine,
    What virtue consecrating every feature!
    Around that neck what dross are gold and pearl!
                              Young's Busiris.

17. She was a form of life and light,
    That, seen, became a part of sight;
    And rose, where'er I turned mine eye,
    The morning-star of memory.
                              Byron's Giaour.

18. Her modest looks the cottage might adorn,
    Sweet as the primrose peeps beneath the thorn.
                              Goldsmith.

19.   The parting lip,
    Like the red rosebud, moist with morning dew,
    Breathing delight.
                              Thomson.

20. She had a woman's mouth with all its pearls complete;
    And for her eyes, what could such eyes do there,
    But weep, and weep, that they were born so fair?
                              Keats.

21. Two of the fairest stars in all the heaven,
    Having some business, do entreat her eyes
    To twinkle in their spheres till they return.
                                    Shakspeare.

22. I see thee graceful, straight, and tall,
    I see thee sweet and bonnie;
    But, oh! what will my torments be,
    If thou refuse thy Johnnie!
                                    Burns.

23. My love is like the red, red rose,
    That's newly sprung in June:
    Oh! my love's like the melody
    That's sweetly played in tune.
                                    Burns.

24. Wi' eager look upon a book,
    You'll aft see lady Ann,
    Wi' jetty locks, an' lily neck
    Bent like a stately swan.
                                    Holmes.

25. Oh! was she but as true as fair,
    'Twad put an end to my despair;
    Instead of that, she is unkind,
    And wavers like the winter wind.
                                    Jockey and Jenny.

26. Her hair is the wing o' the blackbird,
    Her eye is the eye o' the dove,
    Her lips are the ripe blushing rose-bud,
    Her bosom's the palace of love.
                                    Robert Burns, Jr.

27. As bonnié lasses I ha'e seen,
    And mony full as braw,
But for a modest gracefu' mien
    The like I never saw.
                            Burns.

28. Her eyes' dark charm 'twere vain to tell,
    But gaze on that of the gazelle,
    It will assist thy fancy well,
    As large, as languishingly dark,
    But soul beamed forth in every spark.
                            Byron.

29. Her glossy hair was clustered o'er a brow
    Bright with intelligence, and fair and smooth;
Her eyebrow's shape was like the aerial bow,
    Her cheek all purple with the beam of youth,
Mounting at times to a transparent glow,
    As if her veins ran lightning; she, in sooth,
Possessed an air and grace by no means common:
Her stature tall—I hate a dumpy woman.
                            Byron.

30. Here, I can trace the locks of gold,
    Which round thy snowy forehead wave;
The cheeks, which sprung from Beauty's mould,
    The lips, which made me Beauty's slave.
Here, I can trace——ah no! that eye,
    Whose azure floats in liquid fire,
Must all the painter's art defy,
    And bid him from the task retire.
                            Byron.

31. There was an Irish lady, to whose bust
    I ne'er saw justice done, and yet she was
    A frequent model; and if e'er she must
    Yield to stern Time and Nature's wrinkling laws,
    They will destroy a face which mortal thought
    Ne'er compassed, nor less mortal chisel wrought.
    Byron.

32. That form, with eye so dark, and cheek so fair,
    And auburn waves of gemmed and braided hair;
    With shape of fairy lightness.
    Byron.

33. Thy cheek is o' the rose's hue,
        My only jo and dearie, O;
    Thy neck is o' the siller dew
        Upon the bank sae brierie, O.
    Thy teeth are o' the ivory;
    O sweet's the twinkle o' thine e'e:
    Nae joy, nae pleasure, blinks on me,
        My only jo and dearie, O.
    Gall.

34. I wat he ga'e her monie a kiss,
        And Maggie took them nae amiss:
    'Tween ilka smack pleased her wi' this,
        That Bess was but a gawkie.
    Muirhead.

35. Sae flaxen were her ringlets,
        Her eyebrows of a darker hue,
    Bewitchingly o'erarching
        Twa laughing een o' bonnie blue.
    Burns.

36. Nelly's gawsy, saft and gay,
    Fresh as the lucken flowers in May;
    Ilk ane that sees her, cries, Ah hey,
        She's bonny! O I wonder at her.
    The dimples of her chin and cheek,
        And limbs sae plump invite to dawt her;
    Her lips sae sweet, and skin sae sleek,
        Make many mouths beside mine water.
                                    Ramsay.

37. Our Girzy was now thirty-six,
        Though some rather mair did her ca';
    And ane quite sae auld to get married
        Has little or nae chance ava.
    And Girzy, aft thinking on this,
        Lang sighs frae her bosom wad draw;
    Oh, is it not awful to think
        I may not be married ava!
                                    Anon.

38. Miss Bridget Adair lived up one pair of stairs,
        In a street leading out of Soho;
    And though lovely and fair, had seen thirty years,
        Without being blest with a beau.
                                    Old Song.

39. Colour and shape, fair limbs and face,
        Sweetness and wit in all you'll find;
    In motion, speech, in voice, in grace,
        A model here of woman-kind!
                                    Cherry.

40. Her beauteous cheek discloses
    The lily of the spring,
    The vermeil tint of roses,
    And down of cygnet's wing;
    Her envious lid, while sleeping
    Concealed her azure eye;
    Her silken lashes sweeping
    Her cheek of varied dye.
                                Sullivan.

41. Do not my eyes, when I gaze on each feature,
    Express all the transport that reigns in my soul!
    Yes, they avow that I sigh for a creature
    Created by heaven each thought to control.
                                Ireland.

42. Neat Nelly, the milk-maid, in short-waisted gown,
    All the airs of the fashion puts on;
    And emulates all the fine ladies in town,
    As she flirts and coquettes it with John;
    Has the same vapid stare, the same slide, the same bob,
    The same sigh, without feeling or passion;
    With the same rise and fall bids her bosom to throb,
    As the rantipole woman of fashion.
                                Dibdin.

43. Her chin's, sure, a long one, all garnished with
        bristles,
    And, whenever you kiss her, they scratch you like
        thistles;
    Her head a Dutch cheese is, her face a Dutch clock's,
    Her ringlets are carrots—-Och! no, they are golden
        locks.
                                Beuler.

44. Oh! there are looks and tones that dart
    An instant sunshine through the heart;
    As if the soul that minute caught
    Some treasure it through life had sought;
    As if the very lips and eyes,
    Predestined to have all our sighs,
    And never be forgot again,
    Sparkled and spoke before us then.

Moore.

45. The rose of the valley
    Her modest head bowed,
    Though loveliest, seeking
    Her beauties to shroud,
    Beneath the dew bending,
    That clung to the flower,
    Like Beauty, desponding,
    In Misery's hour.

Evans.

46. Her eyes are so black, 'pon my soul, I'm no joker,
    As two holes in a blanket, that's burnt with a poker;
    And, as for their brightness, I'll tell you what's more,
    They're like two scalded gooseberries stuck in a door.

The Irish Beauty.

47. When jetty locks are turned to gray,
    That formed such charms for lovers' hearts;
    When eyes are dim, and scarce can see,
    That beamed such fires, and threw such darts.
    'Tis vain the killing art to try,
    The golden moments are gone by.

Wolcot.

48. The beautiful tints which thy features adorn
     I contrast with the colours of art;
     And exult that in Nature's low valley was born
     My Anna, the pride of my heart.
                                   Old Song.

49. Oh! the witchery that lurks in Fanny's dark eye!
     Such a peculiar tendency shows!
     That 'twere the sex-hater only, when she was nigh,
     Could subdue fond desire as it rose!
                                   L. W. K.

50. Her unbound tresses curling flowed,
     And wantoned with the zephyr;
     Her cheeks with modest crimson glowed,
     'Twas Nature altogether!
     Her sparkling eyes were sunbeams bright,
     Her wit the scourge of folly!
     Her smile was day, her frown dark night;
     Love's queen on earth was Dolly.
                                   Old Song.

Describe the Personal Appearance of Him you love.

Answered by a Lady.

EXAMINE every several lineament,
And see how one another lends content;
And what obscured in this fair volume lies,
Find written in the margin of his eyes.
This precious book of love, this unbound lover,
To beautify him, only lacks a cover.
Shakspeare.

2. The first of my lovers was a swaggering blade,
To rattle the thundering drum was his trade;
His leg was so tight and his cheek was so ruddy,
Transported I was with my soger laddie.
Burns.

3. He had an English look; that is, was square
In make, of a complexion white and ruddy,
Good teeth, with curling rather dark-brown hair,
And, it might be from thought, or toil, or study,
An open brow a little marked with care.
Byron.

44

4. See whàt a grace was seated on his brow:
Hyperion's curls; the front of Jove himself;
An eye like Mars, to threaten and command;
A station, like the herald Mercury,
New-lighted on a heaven-kissing hill;
A combination, and a form, indeed,
Where every god did seem to set his seal,
To give the world assurance of a man.
Shakspeare.

5. No haughty gesture marks his gait,
No pompous tone his word,
No studied attitude is seen,
No palling nonsense heard.
Eliza Cook.

6. His high broad forehead, marble fair,
Told of the power of thought within;
And strength was in his raven hair—
But when he smiled, a spell was there
That more than strength or power could win.
Mrs. Hale's Vigil of Love.

7. The seal of truth is on thy gallant form,
For none but cowards lie.
Murphy's Alonzo.

8. How many cowards, whose hearts are all as false
As stairs of sand, wear upon their chins
The beards of Hercules, and frowning Mars,
Who, inward search'd, have livers white as milk?
Shakspeare.

9. 'Twas pretty, though a plague,
   To see him every hour; to sit and draw
   His arched brows, his hawking eye, his curls,
   In our heart's table.
                                    Shakspeare.

10. His wig was weel pouther'd, as good as when new,
    His waistcoat was white, his coat it was blue;
    He put on a ring, a sword, and cocked hat—
    And who could refuse the Laird wi' a' that?
                                    Miss Ferrier.

11. His features, pale, and beautiful
    As those of the old statues, and with much
    Of the ideal tenderness that breathed
    Around the marble, till it rivalled life—
    Yet with a latent sternness, lurking still
    About the august high forehead, and the lip,
    And the fine sweeping profile, that recalled
    Yet more a statue's strong similitude.
                                    Sisters of the West.

12. I saw in the morn the reaper bold—
       The reaper of the plain,
    Above his brow were locks of gold,
       The hue of the ripened grain;
    His eye was as blue as the sky that threw
       Its light on his waving field,
    And his voice was soft as the winds that blew
       To make the harvest yield.
                                    Sisters of the West.

13. I know not why I loved that man,
    More than a guiding star;
His frame was worn, his cheek was wan,
    And marked by sun and scar.
           Sisters of the West.

14. The expectancy and rose of the fair state,
The glass of fashion, and the mould of form—
The observed of all observers!
           Shakspeare.

15. And even now I see him by my side,
Stately as princes should be; with those eyes,
Boundless and deep as the unfathomed skies,
Gazing on me, with flashing orbs of pride.
           Sisters of the West.

16.   That brow all calm and high;
    That dark and radiant eye;
That raven hair, in its rich glossy fold;
    That smile, whose radiant beams
    Were like the rainbow gleams,
Lighting a sky that else were dark and cold.
           Sisters of the West.

17. Oh! thou art strangely altered! and thy face
    With the deep lines of care and wo all fraught;
And even the channel of thy tears we trace,
    And on thy brow the scathing work of thought!
           Sisters of the West.

18. His proud eye wears the eagle's look;
    His cap, the eagle's plume;—
           Sisters of the West.

19. Tall, slenderly, yet nobly formed; endowed
    With grace, and gentleness, and stately ease;
                    Sisters of the West.

20.   Don't think that I chose
          My love for his nose,
    Cheeks cherry, or peepers blue;
          But truly I sees, a maiden to please,
    A certain something in you.
                              Old Song.

21. He's tall and he's straight as the poplar-tree,
          His cheeks are as fresh as the rose;
    He looks like a squire of high degree,
          When drest in his Sunday clothes.
                              Mrs. Brooke.

22. And then he had good looks; that point was carried
          Nem. con. amongst the women.
                              Byron.

23. His tender smiles, love's day-dawn on his lips!
    That spiritual and almost heavenly light
    In his commanding eye—his mien heroic,
    Virtue's own native heraldry!
                              Coleridge.

24. He looked very like a tea-kettle,
    He looked very like a tea-kettle,
    But he couldn't sing half so well.
                              Manager Strut.

25. The empty coxcomb which you chose,
   Just like the flower of day,
   Shook by each wind that folly blows,
   Seems born to flutter and decay.
                              Dibdin.

26. Spanking Jack was so comely, so pleasant, so jolly,
   Though winds blew great guns, still he'd whistle
       and sing.
                              Dibdin.

27. Anxiety for thee, love,
   Has marked my brow with care,
   The heart once blithe and free, love,
    Lives a victim to despair.
                            Westmacott.

28. Sighed she, "I love this officer, although his nose
     is red,
   And his legs are what his regiment call bandy, oh!"
                            Colman.

29. A Dandy is like, who can say
   What a Dandy is like, who can say?
                            Old Song.

30. Then I put on my whiskers, mustachios, and wig,
   And waistcoat adorned with a lavender-sprig;
   With rings on my fingers, and patch on my chin,
   I walked through the streets with a beautiful grin:
     I was scented with musk and with roses,
     And smelt like a bundle of posies,
     The passengers sniffed up their noses,
      And cried, "What a beautiful man!"
                            Beuler.

            4

31. Though a barber has never yet mowed my chin,
    With my great broad sword I long to begin.
                                    O'Keefe.

32. He was, to weet, a little roguish page,
    Save sleep and play who minded naught at all,
    Like most the untaught striplings of his age.
                                    Thomson.

33. Straight from the filth of this low grub, behold!
    Comes fluttering forth a gaudy spendthrift heir,
    All glossy gay, enamelled all with gold.
    The silly tenant of the summer air,
    In folly lost, of nothing takes he care.
                                    Thomson.

34. There was a man of special grave remark;
    A certain tender gloom o'erspread his face,
    Pensive, not sad; in thought involved, not dark.
                                    Thomson.

35. A joyous youth, who took you at first sight;
    Him the wild wave of pleasure hither drove,
    Before the sprightly tempest-tossing light:
    Certes, he was a most engaging wight.
                                    Thomson.

36. Of feature stern, Selvaggio well yclep'd,
    A rough, unpolished man, robust and bold.
                                    Thomson.

37. He crept along, unpromising of mien.
    Gross he who judges so.   His soul was fair,
    Bright as the children of yon azure sheen!
    True comeliness, which nothing can impair,
    Dwells in the mind: all else is vanity and glare.
                                        Thomson.

38. Of morbid hue his features, sunk and sad;
    His hollow eyne shook forth a sickly light,
    And o'er his lank jawbone, in piteous plight,
    His black rough beard was matted rank and vile.
                                        Thomson.

39. Mislike me not for my complexion,
    The shadowed livery of the burnished sun,
    To whom I am a neighbour, and near bred.
                                        Shakspeare.

40. Thou art too wild, too rude, and bold of voice;—
    Parts that become thee happily enough,
    And in such eyes as ours appear not faults:
    But where thou art not known, why, there they show
    Something too liberal.
                                        Shakspeare.

41. So are those crisped snaky golden locks,
    Which make such wanton gambols with the wind,
    Upon supposed fairness, often known
    To be the dowry of a second head,
    The skull that bred them in the sepulchre.
                                        Shakspeare.

42. 'Tis not your inky brows, your black-silk hair,
   Your bugle eyeballs, nor your cheek of cream,
   That can entame my spirits to your worship.
                                        Shakspeare.

43.   Not very pretty:—
   But, sure, he's proud; and yet his pride becomes him:
   He'll make a proper man: The best thing in him
   Is his complexion.
                                        Shakspeare.

44. And high top bald with dry antiquity,
   A wretched ragged man, o'ergrown with hair.
                                        Shakspeare.

45. A traitor you do look like; but such traitors
   His majesty seldom fears.
                                        Shakspeare.

46.   Dear lad, believe it;
   For they shall yet belie thy happy years,
   That say, thou art a man: Diana's lip
   Is not more smooth, and rubious; thy small pipe
   Is as the maiden's organ, shrill and sound,
   And all is semblative a woman's part.
                                        Shakspeare.

47. In voices well divulged, free, learned, and valiant;
   And, in dimension, and the shape of nature,
   A gracious person.
                                        Shakspeare.

48. Thy tongue, thy face, thy limbs, actions, and spirit,
   Do give thee five-fold blazon.
                                        Shakspeare.

49. O, what a deal of scorn looks beautiful
    In the contempt and anger of his lip!
                                   Shakspeare.

50. Your face, my thane, is as a book, where men
    May read strange matters:—To beguile the time,
    Look like the time; bear welcome in your eye,
    Your hand, your tongue: look like the innocent
         flower,
    But be the serpent under it.
                                   Shakspeare.

What is the Character of your Lady-love?

Answered by a Gentleman.

ILD as the infant rose, and innocent
As when Heaven lent her us. Her mind as well
As face, is yet a paradise untainted
With blemishes, or the spreading weeds of vice.
Robert Baron's Mirza.

2. Accomplishments were native to her mind,
    Like precious pearls within a clasping shell,
And winning grace her every act refined,
    Like sunshine shedding beauty where it fell.
Mrs. Hale.

3. She glares in balls, front boxes, and the ring,
A vain, unquiet, glittering, wretched thing!
Pride, pomp, and state but reach her outward part;
She sighs,—and is no duchess at her heart.
Pope.

4. Devoted, anxious, generous, void of guile,
And with her whole heart's welcome in her smile.
Mrs. Norton.

"She has a glowing heart, they say."

Lady's Oracle, p. 55.

5. Within the oyster's shell uncouth
   The purest pearl may hide : —
   Trust me you'll find a heart of truth
   Within that rough outside.

   Mrs. Osgood.

6. She has a glowing heart, they say,
   Though calm her seeming be;
   And oft that warm heart's lovely play
   Upon her cheek I see.

   Mrs. Osgood.

7. Not soon provoked, however stung and teased,
   And, if perhaps made angry, soon appeased;
   She rather waives than will dispute her right,
   And, injured, makes forgiveness her delight.

   Cowper's Charity.

8. Beneath the cares of earth she does not bow,
   Though she hath ofttimes drained its bitter cup;
   But ever wanders on with heavenward brow,
   And eyes whose lovely orbs are lifted up!

   Mrs. Welby.

9. Self-flattered, unexperienced, high in hope.

   Young.

10. Shall it not be scorn to me
    To harp on such a mouldered string?
    I am shamed through all my nature
    To have loved so slight a thing.

    Tennyson.

11.   Leave her to Heaven,
And to those thorns that in her bosom lodge,
To prick and sting her.
Shakspeare.

12. Her poverty was glad; her heart content,
Nor knew she what the spleen or vapours meant.
Dryden.

13. With every pleasing, every prudent part,
Say, " what can Chloe want ?"—she wants a heart.
She speaks, behaves, and acts just as she ought;
But never, never reach'd one generous thought.
Pope.

14. She is a woman, therefore may be wooed:
She is a woman, therefore may be won.
Shakspeare.

15. She, proud to rule, yet strangely framed to tease,
Neglects his offers while her airs she plays,
Shoots scornful glances from the bended frown,
In brisk disorder trips it up and down.
Parnell.

16.   ke a lovely tree
She grew to woman od, and between whiles
Rejected several su just to learn
How to accept a bette n his turn.
Byron.

17. O serpent heart, hid with a flowering face !
Did ever dragon keep so fair a cave ?
Shakspeare.

18.   She is peevish, sullen, froward,
Proud, disobedient, stubborn, lacking duty.
Shakspeare.

19.   In her youth
There is a prone and speechless dialect,
Such as moves men; besides she hath prosperous art,
When she will play with reason and discourse,
And well she can persuade.
Shakspeare.

20. And if she hapt of any good to heare,
That had to any happily betid,
Then would she inly fret, and grieve, and teare
Her flesh for felnesse, which she inward hid.
Spenser.

21. Ah! doomed indeed to worse than death,
To teach those sweet lips hourly guile;
To breathe through life but falsehood's breath,
And smile with falsehood's smile!
Mrs. Osgood.

22.   She is as constant as the stars
That never vary, and more chaste than they.
Proctor.

23. You are too busy, and too stirring, to
Be put in action; your curiosity
Would do as much harm in a kingdom, as
A monkey in a glass shop; move, and remove,
Till you had broken all.
Cartwright.

24. I have ease, and I have health,
   And I have spirits light as air;
And more than wisdom, more than wealth—
A merry heart that laughs at care.
H. H. Milman.

25. The meek mountain daisy, with delicate crest,
And the violet whose eye told the heaven of her
    breast.
Mrs. Sigourney.

26.   Your heart
Is crammed with arrogancy, spleen, and pride.
Shakspeare.

27. The dust on the blossom,
   The spray on the sea—
Ay, ask thine own bosom—
   Are emblems of thee.
Miss Landon.

28. Her manners, by the world refined,
Left all the taint of modish vice behind,
And made each charm of polished courts agree
With candid truth's simplicity.
Lyttleton.

29.   Hadst thou seen
How in each motion her most innocent soul
Beamed forth and brightened, thou thyself wouldst
    tell me,
Guilt is a thing impossible in her!
Coleridge.

30. All fancy sick she is, and pale of cheer
    With sighs of love.
                             Shakspeare.

31. Desires composed, affections ever even;
    Tears that delight, and sighs that waft to heaven:
    Grace shines around her with serenest beams,
    And whispering angels prompt her golden dreams.
                                 Pope.

32. Dorinda's sparkling wit and eyes
    United cast too fierce a light;
    Which blazes high, but quickly dies,
    Pains not the heart, but hurts the sight.
                          Earl of Dorset.

33. Seraph of heaven! too gentle to be human,
    Veiling beneath that radiant form of woman
    All that is insupportable in thee
    Of light, and love, and immortality!
                             Shelley.

34. A shadow of some golden dream; a Splendor
    Leaving the third sphere pilotless; a tender
    Reflection of the eternal Moon of Love,
    Under whose motions life's dull billows move;
    A Metaphor of Spring and Youth and Morning;
    A Vision like incarnate April, warning,
    With smiles and tears, Frost the Anatomy
    Into his summer grave.
                             Shelley.

35. In many mortal forms I rashly sought
    The shadow of that idol of my thought.
    And some were fair—but beauty dies away:
    Others were wise—but honied words betray:
    And one was true.
                       Shelley.

36. And underneath that face, like summer's ocean's,
    Its lip as moveless, and its cheek as clear,
    Slumbers a whirlwind of the heart's emotions,
    Love, hatred, pride, hope, sorrow—all save fear.
                       Halleck.

37. Nature has cast me in so soft a mould,
    That but to hear a story, feigned for pleasure,
    Of some sad lover's death, moistens my eyes.
                       Dryden.

38. Each witchery of soul and sense,
    Enshrined in angel innocence,
    Combined to frame the fatal spell—
    That blest—and broke my heart—Farewell!
                       Pringle.

39.   Around her shone
    The light of love, the purity of grace,
    The mind, the music breathing from her face;
    The heart whose softness harmonized the whole.
                       Byron.

40. Thou turn'st mine eyes into my very soul,
    And there I see such black and grained spots,
    As will not leave their tinct.
                       Shakspeare.

41. A delicate, frail thing,—but made
For spring sunshine, or summer shade.
A slender flower, unmeet to bear
One April shower,—so slight, so fair.
Miss Landon.

42. Though time thy bloom is stealing,
There's still beyond his art
The wild-flower wreath of feeling,
The sunbeam of the heart.
Halleck.

43. Sincerity's my chief delight,
The darling pleasure of the mind.
Lady Chudleigh.

44. Wine may indeed excite the meekest dame;
But keen Xantippe, scorning borrowed flame,
Cant vent her thunders, and her lightnings play,
O'er cooling gruel and composing tea.
Young.

45. Thy talk is the sweet extract of all speech,
And holds mine ear in blissful slavery.
Bailey.

46. Priestess of falsehood—deeply learned
In all heart-treachery!
Sara J. Clarke.

47. Thy likeness, thy fit help, thy other self,
Thy wish exactly to thy heart's desire.
Milton.

48. All day, like some sweet bird, content to sing
    In its small cage, she moveth to and fro—
    And ever and anon will upward spring
    To her sweet lips, fresh from the fount below,
    The murmured melody of pleasant thought,
    Light household duties, evermore inwrought.
                        Mrs. E. Oakes Smith.

49. 'Tis beauty that doth oft make women proud:
    But, God he knows, thy share thereof is small:
    'Tis virtue that doth make them most admired;
    The contrary doth make thee wondered at.
                        Shakspeare.

50. I am a woman! nay, a woman wronged!
    And when our sex from injuries take fire,
    Our softness turns to fury—and our thoughts
    Breathe vengeance and destruction.
                        Savage.

What is the Character of Him you love?

Answered by a Lady.

HE was a man of a strange temperament,
Of mild demeanour, though of savage mood,
Moderate in all his habits, and content
With temperance in pleasure as in food,
Quick to perceive, and strong to bear, and meant
For something better, if not wholly good;
His country's wrongs and his despair to save her
Had stung him from a slave to an enslaver.
Byron.

2. Old king Coul was a jolly old soul,
    And a jolly old soul was he;
And old king Coul he had a brown bowl,
    And they brought him in fiddlers three.
Old Song.

3. The friend of man, the friend of truth,
The friend of age, and guide of youth;
Few hearts like his with virtue warmed,
Few heads with knowledge so informed.
Burns.
63

4. His nature is too noble for the world:
   He would not flatter Neptune for his trident,
   Or Jove for his power to thunder. His heart's his
      mouth:
   What his breast forges, that his tongue must vent;
   And, being angry, does forget that ever
   He heard the name of death.
                       . *Shakspeare.*

5. He hath a tear for pity, and a hand
   Open as day, for melting charity:
   Yet, notwithstanding, being incensed, he's flint;
   As humorous as winter, and as sudden
   As flaws congealed in the spring of day.
                       Shakspeare.

6. Trust not a man: we are by nature false,
   Dissembling, subtle, cruel, and inconstant;
   When a man talks of love, with caution hear him,
   But if he swears he'll certainly deceive thee.
                       Otway.

7. When all thy mountains clap their hands in joy,
   And all thy cataracts thunder—"That's the boy!"
                       O. W. Holmes.

8. It is too full o' the milk of human kindness
   To catch the nearest way; thou wouldst be great;
   Art not without ambition; but without
   The illness should attend it: what thou wouldst
      highly,
   That wouldst thou holily: wouldst not play false,
   And yet wouldst wrongly win.
                       Shakspeare.

9. The churl who holds its heresy to *think*,
Who loves no music but the dollar's clink,
Who laughs to scorn the wisdom of the schools,
And deems the first of poets first of fools.
Sprague.

10. Not all the pumice of the polished town
Can smooth the roughness of the barnyard clown;
Rich, honoured, titled, he betrays his race
By this one mark—he's awkward in his face.
O. W. Holmes.

11. An honest mind and plain,—he must speak truth;
An they will take it, so; if not, he's plain.
These kind of knaves I know, which in this plain-
ness
Harbour more craft, and far corrupter ends,
Than twenty silly ducking observants,
That stretch their duty nicely.
Shakspeare.

12. A mad-cap ruffian, and a swearing jack,
That thinks with oaths to face the matter out.
Shakspeare.

13. I'd rather be a dog, and bay the moon,
Than such a Roman.
Shakspeare.

14. He'll suit his bearing to the hour,
Laugh, listen, learn, or teach,
With joyous freedom in his mirth
And candour in his speech.
Eliza Cook.

5

15. When better cherries are not to be had,
    We needs must take the seeming best of bad.
                                    Daniel.

16. Drawn by conceit from reason's plan,
    How vain is that poor creature, man!
    How pleased is every paltry elf
    To prate about that thing, himself.
                                    Churchill.

17. I am constant as the northern star;
    Of whose true, fixed, and resting quality
    There is no fellow in the firmament.
                                    Shakspeare.

18. Go, prick thy face, and over-red thy fear,
    Thou lily-livered boy.   What soldiers, patch?
    Death of thy soul, those linen cheeks of thine
    Are counsellors to fear.   What soldiers, whey-face?
                                    Shakspeare.

19.   This is he,
    That kissed his hand away in courtesy;
    This is the ape of form, Monsieur the nice,
    That when he plays at tables, chides the dice
    In honourable terms.
                                    Shakspeare.

20. The over curious are not over wise.
                                    Massinger.

21.   Much had he read,
    Much more had seen: he studied from the life,
    And in the original perused mankind.
                                    Armstrong.

22. The ghost of many a veteran bill
    Shall hover around his slumbers.
                              O. W. Holmes.

23. The politic, the factious fool,
    The busy, buzzing, talking, hardened knave;
    The quaint smooth rogue, that sins against his reason,
    Calls saucy loud sedition public zeal:
    And mutiny the dictates of his spirit.
                              Otway.

24.   If at home, sir,
    He's all my exercise, my mirth, my matter:
    Now my sworn friend, and then mine enemy:
    My parasite, my soldier, statesman, all.
                              Shakspeare.

25. Behold! his breakfasts shine with reputation!
    His dinners are the wonder of the nation!
    With these he treats both commoners and quality,
    Who praise, where'er they go, his hospitality.
                              Wolcot.

26. His words are bonds, his oaths are oracles;
    His love sincere, his thoughts immaculate;
    His tears pure messengers sent from his heart;
    His heart as far from fraud as heaven and earth.
                              Shakspeare.

27. His fiery temper brooks not opposition,
    And must be met with soft and supple arts,
    With crouching courtesy, and honied words,
    Such as assuage the fierce, and bend the strong.
                              Rowe.

28. Nothing exceeds in ridicule, no doubt,
    A fool *in* fashion, but a fool that's *out;*
    His passion for absurdity's so strong,
    He cannot bear a rival in the wrong.
                    Young.

29.   Lord Angelo is precise;
    Stands at a guard with envy; scarce confesses
    That his blood flows, that his appetite
    Is more to bread than stone.
                    Shakspeare.

30. She hath sealed thee for herself: for thou hast been
    As one, in suffering all, that suffers nothing;
    A man, that fortune's buffets and rewards
    Hast ta'en with equal thanks.
                    Shakspeare.

31. They say that he has genius. I but see
      That he gets wisdom as the flower gets hue,
    While others hive it like the toiling bee;
      That with him all things beautiful keep new.
                    Willis.

32. He is a noble gentleman; withal
    Happy in's endeavours: the general voice
    Sounds him for courtesy, behaviour, language,
    And every fair demeanour, an example.
                    John Ford.

33. Fat paunches have lean pates; and dainty bits
    Make rich the ribs, but bankrupt quite the wits.
                    Shakspeare.

34. God gave him reverence of laws,
    Yet stirring blood in freedom's cause—
    A spirit to the rocks akin,
    The eye of the hawk and the fire therein.
                                Coleridge.

35. I know thee for a man of many thoughts,
    And deeds of good and ill, extreme in both
    Fatal and fated in thy sufferings.
                                Byron.

36.   His honour's linked
    Unto his life; he that will seek the one
    Must venture for the other or lose both.
                                Tatham.

37. My master is of churlish disposition,
    And little recks to find the way to heaven
    By doing deeds of hospitality.
                                Shakspeare.

38. A villain with a smiling cheek:
    A goodly apple, rotten at the heart:
    O, what a goodly outside falsehood hath!
                                Shakspeare.

39. From worldly cares himself he did esloin,
    And greatly shunned manly exercise;
    From every work he challenged essoin,
    For contemplation' sake.
                                Spenser.

40. He that has but impudence,
     To all things has a fair pretence;
     And put among his wants but shame,
     To all the world may lay his claim.

Butler.

41. He hath a person, and a smooth dispose,
     To be suspected; framed to make women false.

Shakspeare.

42. He cannot e'en essay to walk sedate,
     But in his very gait one sees a jest,
     That's ready to break out in spite of all
     His seeming.

Knowles.

43. A man of law, a man of peace,
     To frame a contract or a lease.

Crabbe.

44. This fellow's of exceeding honesty,
     And knows all qualities, with a learned spirit,
     Of human things.

Shakspeare.

45. Merit like his, the fortune of the mind,
     Beggars all wealth.

Thomson.

46. I pity bashful men, who feel the pain
     Of fancied scorn and undeserved disdain,
     And bear the marks upon a blushing face
     Of needless shame and self-imposed disgrace.

Cowper.

47. I do remember an apothecary,—
And hereabouts he dwells,—whom late I noted
In tattered weeds, with overwhelming brows,
Culling of simples; meagre were his looks,
Sharp misery had worn him to the bones.

Shakspeare.

48. My purse is very slim, and very few
   The acres that I number;
But I am seldom stupid, never blue;
My riches are an honest heart and true,
   And quiet slumber.

Epes Sargent.

49.   'Tis much he dares;
And, to that dauntless temper of his mind,
He hath a wisdom that doth guide his valour
To act in safety.

Shakspeare

50. Ah! sly deceiver; branded o'er and o'er,
   Yet still believed! exulting o'er the wreck
Of sober vows.

Armstrong.

How do you pass your Time?

Answered by a Gentleman.

WHY do you keep alone,
    Of sorriest fancies your companions making;
    Using those thoughts, which should indeed
        have died
    With them they think on?
                                    Shakspeare.

2. Nor the sail high heaving waters o'er,
    Nor the rural dance on the moonlight shore,—
    Can the wild and fearless joy exceed
    Of a fearless leap on a fiery steed.
                                    Sara J. Clarke.

3. Lived in his saddle, loved the chase, the course,
    And always, e'er he mounted, kissed his horse.
                                    Cowper.

4. Unhappy man! whom sorrow thus and rage
    To different ills alternately engage;
    Who drinks, alas! but to forget.
                                    Prior.

72

5. From worldly cares himself he did esloin,
   And greatly shunned manly exercise;
   From every work he challenged essoin,
   For contemplation' sake.
                                    Spenser.

6. Come and trip it as you go,
   On the light fantastic toe,
   And in thy right hand lead with thee
   The mountain nymph, sweet liberty.
                                    Milton.

7. I've pored o'er many a yellow page
   Of ancient wisdom, and have won,
   Perchance, a scholar's name.
                              G. W. Bethune.

8. Give me some music; music moody food
   For us that trade in love.
                              Shakspeare.

9. He capers nimbly in a lady's chamber,
   To the lascivious pleasing of a lute.
                              Shakspeare.

10. Here the rude clamour of the sportman's joy,
    The gun fast thundering, and the winded horns,
    Would tempt the muse to sing the rural game.
                                    Thomson.

11. There at the foot of yonder nodding beech,
    That wreaths its old fantastic roots so high,
    His listless length at noontide would he stretch,
    And pore upon the brook that bubbles by.
                                    Gray.

12. But midst the crowd, the hum, the shock of men.

> *Byron.*

13. He goes to the river side,—
    Nor hook nor line hath he:
    He stands in the meadows wide,—
    Nor gun nor scythe to see.

> *Ralph W. Emerson.*

14. Shun such as lounge through afternoons and eves,
    And on thy dial write—"Beware of thieves!"
    Felon of minutes, never taught to feel
    The worth of treasures which thy fingers steal.

> *O. W. Holmes.*

15. This is a traveller, sir; knows men and manners.

> *Beaumont and Fletcher.*

16. My book o' grace I'll try to read,
    Though conned wi' little skill.

> *Joanna Baillie.*

17. I rather would entreat thy company,
    To see the wonders of the world abroad,
    Than living dully sluggardized at home.

> *Shakspeare.*

18. I've trod the glittering way
    Of the land through, and lived in brightest halls.

> *G. Mellen.*

19. Why I, in this weak piping time of peace,
Have no delight to pass away the time;
Unless to spy my shadow in the sun.
Shakspeare.

20. Not sleeping, to engross his idle body,
But praying, to enrich his watchful soul.
Shakspeare

21. To-night, we'll wander through the streets, and note
The qualities of people.
Shakspeare.

22. He fishes, drinks, and wastes
The lamps of night in revel.
Shakspeare.

23. Let the world heave on with its ocean-noise,
I ask but friends and home.
G. Mellen.

24. No care, no stop: so senseless of expense,
That he will neither know how to maintain it,
Nor cease his flow of riot; takes no account
How things go from him.
Shakspeare.

25.   Breaks scurril jests;
And with ridiculous and awkward action
(Which, slanderer, he imitation calls)
He pageants us.
Shakspeare.

26. I veil my brow from this dim earth,
    And dream of brighter spheres;
I muse by my forsaken hearth
    Of time unmarked by years.
                  Sisters of the West.

27. Gazing on thy blue eyes, and tendril hair;
Here, even here, my spirit's depths unclosing,
I'll breathe to thee the tale of my despair.
                  Sisters of the West.

28. We'll watch the white and leaping spray,
    Hurled from our cleaving prow;
And the wild breeze shall kiss away
    The soft locks from each brow.
                  Sisters of the West.

29. Oh! love like mine hath lonely dreams,
    And clinging doubts and fears.
                  Sisters of the West.

30. And thou art like that God-struck man,
    Forever wandering on;
Thy spirit's doom is weird and wan;
    Alone! alone! alone!
                  Sisters of the West

31. Inspiring, bold John Barleycorn!
What dangers thou canst make us scorn.
                  Burns.

32. Beneath the silver-gleaming ray,
'To mark the mutual kindling eye.
                  Burns.

33. Would you be a man of fashion,
    Would you lead a life divine,
    Take a little dram of passion
    In a lusty dose of wine.
                  Anon.

34. The fat shining glutton looks up to his shelf.
                  Garrick.

35. Oh! sweet 'tis to list to the nightingale's note,
    Or watch the moon play through yon bushes,
    Or hark to the sound of the silver-toned lute,
    Or the white wave, down the rough steep that
        gushes.
                  Bruton.

36. He'll drink and he'll fight, and a joke's his delight;
    Good humour attends him.
                  Beuler.

37. I make all look so handsome, so charming my
        trade is,
    And neatly I tickle the taste of the ladies.
                  Crow.

38. May the pedant be lost in his phantom pursuit,
    While I revel in wine, and with bumpers recruit;
    Since the wisest can never perfection attain,
    Why should life proffer sweets and enjoyments in
        vain?
                  Old Song.

39. To the woods and the fields, my brave boys, haste
      away!
    Our sport is to follow the hare;
    For the morning is clear, and delightfully gay,
    Sure nothing with this can compare!
                                        Old Song.

40. Electioneering, privateering—
    Auctioneering, volunteering.
                                        Old Song.

41. I've seen some balls and revels in my time,
      And staid them over for some silly reason,
    And then I looked (I hope it was no crime)
      To see what lady best stood out the season.
                                        Byron.

42. Sermons he read, and lectures he endured,
      And homilies, and lives of all the saints;
    To Jerome and to Chrysostom inured,
      He did not take such studies for restraints.
                                        Byron.

43. He pored upon the leaves, and on the flowers,
      And heard a voice in all the winds; and then
    He thought of wood-nymphs and immortal bowers,
      And how the goddesses came down to men.
                                        Byron.

44. For my part, I'm a moderate minded bard,
      Fond of a little love, (which I call leisure;)
    I care not for new pleasures, as the old
    Are quite enough for me, so they but hold.
                                        Byron.

45. Here was no lack of innocent diversion
    For the imagination or the senses,
    Song, dance, wine, music, stories from the Persian,
    All pretty pastime in which no offence is.
                                        Byron.

46. He always is complaining of his lot,
    Forsooth, scarce fit for ballads in the street.
                                        Byron.

47. A neat, snug study on a winter's night,
    A book, friend, single lady, or a glass
    Of claret, sandwich, and an appetite,
    Are things which make a pleasant evening pass.
                                        Byron.

48. He now was growing up like a green tree, able
    For love, war, or ambition, which reward
    Their luckier votaries, till old age's tedium
    Make some prefer the circulating medium.
                                        Byron.

49. An old maid of threescore
    For cats and birds more penchant ne'er displayed,
    Although he was not old, nor even a maid.
                                        Byron.

How do you pass your Time?

Answered by a Lady.

BY day she seeks some melancholy shade,
 To hide her sorrow from the prying world;
 At night she watches all the long, long hours,
 And listens to the winds and beating rain,
 With sighs as loud, and tears that fall as fast.

Rowe.

2. I will wash my ploughman's hose,
   And I will dress his o'erlay,
 I will make my ploughman's bed,
   And cheer him late and early.

Burns.

3. But we maun ha'e linen, and that maun ha'e we,
   And how get we that but by spinnin' o't?
 How can we ha'e face for to seek a great fee,
   Except we can help at the winnin' o't?

Ross.

80

4. Wi' love and mirth and social glee
   We'll still keep up the jovial spree,
   While time on wings o' joy shall flee.
                                    Stirrat.

5. When tired wi' her cantraps, she lies in her bed,
   The wark a' neglecket, the house ill up-red,
   When a' our guid neighbours are stirring right early.
                                    Baillie.

6. The dearest enjoyments of home are there,
   The chat and the laugh by the hearth's cheering glare,
   When day and its labours are done.
                                    Smibert.

7. Now I am at my last prayers,
      I pray on baith nicht and day;
   And, oh! if a beggar wad come,
      With that same beggar I'd gae.
   And, oh! and what'll come o' me?
      And, oh! and what'll I do?
   That sic a braw lassie as I
      Should die for a wooer, I trow!
                                    Ramsay.

8. When evening brings its shady hour
      Then who so blithe as we?
   The lamp of love in barn and bower
      Lights up a scene of glee;
   Old Time forgets his running sand
      And joins our roundelay.
                                    Macdonald.

6

9. Hale books I've wrote, both prose and verse,
   And many a rousing dedication.
                                    Chambers' Journal.

10. As Jenny sat down wi' her wheel by the fire,
    An' thought o' the time that was fast fleein' by'er,
    She said to hersel' wi' a heavy hoch hie,
    Oh! a' body's like to be married but me.
                                    Gray.

11. Tear my bright hair, and scratch my praised cheeks;
    Crack my clear voice with sobs and break my heart.
                                    Shakspeare.

12. I must not think of him: I'll call
       Around me dance and song;
    Until this lone dismantled hall
       Shakes with the motley throng.
                                    Sisters of the West.

13. I love those legends, gray
       With venerable years;
    They have a power to sway
       My mood to smiles and tears.
                                    Sisters of the West.

14. Touch thou this lute,
       That, o'er land and sea,
    Its chords, though mute,
       May be signs of thee.
                                    Sisters of the West.

15. Even as I sit and dream alone
    Within this antique hall,
    With its dim echoing floor of stone,
    Its dark empanelled wall.
    Sisters of the West.

16.   In the hall
    I was the light of the festival;
    Tell him, how proudly I paced the dance—
    What powers I bore in a word or glance.
    Sisters of the West.

17.   Fast wanes the heavy time;
    Past is the summer's prime;
    Still doth the lady dream, and watch, and weep.
    Sisters of the West.

18. That song, that song of olden time,
    I fain would hear again;
    The sweeping tone, the measured chime,
    And now the pealing strain.
    Sisters of the West.

19. Oh! while across mine inner sight
    This tide of anguish streams,
    My life is but a darkened night,
    And full of mournful dreams!
    Sisters of the West.

20. Oh! often in the quiet night she sitteth,
    Shedding wild tears, beside the winter hearth;
    While o'er her face the uncertain firelight flitteth;
    Yet darker still is her unmeaning mirth.
    Sisters of the West.

21. In vain my lyre would lightly breathe
  The smile that sorrow fain would wear,
 But mocks the wo that lurks beneath,
  Like roses o'er a sepulchre.
          Byron.

22. For madam's will at nothing stops,
 She must have balls, and routs, and fops,
 And often ransack all the shops,
  In gay attire to robe her.
          Dibdin.

23. Hence, all ye vain delights,
 As short as are the nights
 Wherein you spend your folly!
      Beaumont and Fletcher.

24. I feel like one who treads alone
  Some banquet-hall deserted,
 Whose lights are fled, whose garlands dead,
  And all but he departed.
         T. Moore.

25. She strove the neighbourhood to please
  With manners wondrous winning;
 And never followed wicked ways,
  Unless when she was sinning.
        Goldsmith.

26. Ye that are basking in Pleasure's gay beam,
 Ye that are sailing on Hope's golden stream,
 A cloud may come o'er ye—a wave sweep the deck.
        Planche.

27. Talking, she knew not why and cared not what,
So that her female friends, with envy broiling,
Beheld her airs and triumph, and all that.
Byron.

28. Endearing waltz—to thy more melting tune
Bow, Irish jig, and ancient rigadoon;
Scotch reels, avaunt! and country-dance, forego
Your future claims to each fantastic toe.
Byron.

29. She kept a journal, where his faults were noted;
And opened certain trunks of books and letters,
All which might, if occasion served, be quoted.
Byron.

30. The gentle pressure, and the thrilling touch,
The least glance better understood than words,
Which still said all, and ne'er could say too much;
A language, too, but like to that of birds.
Byron.

31. The truth is, I've grown lately rather phthisical:
I don't know what the reason is—the air,
Perhaps; but as I suffer from the shocks
Of illness, I grow much more orthodox.
Byron.

32. High in high circles, gentle in her own,
She was the mild reprover of the young,
Whenever—which means every day—they'd shown
An awkward inclination to go wrong.
Byron.

33. The elderly walked through the library,
    And tumbled books, or criticised the pictures,
Or sauntered through the gardens piteously,
    And made upon the hothouse several strictures.
                                    Byron.

34. Observant of the foibles of the crowd,
    Yet ne'er betraying this in conversation.
                                    Byron.

35. She gazed upon a world she scarcely knew,
    As seeking not to know it; silent, lone,
As grows a flower, thus quietly she grew,
    And kept her heart serene within its zone.
                                    Byron.

36. Faults which attract because they are not tame;
    Follies tricked out so brightly that they blind:—
These seals upon her wax made no impression,
    Such was her coldness or her self-possession.
                                    Byron.

37. Though too well-bred to quiz men to their faces,
    Her laughing blue eyes with a glance could seize
The ridicules of people in all places—
    That honey of your fashionable bees—
And store it up for mischievous enjoyment.
                                    Byron.

38. Much on my early youth I love to dwell,
    Ere yet I bade that friendly dome farewell,
    Where first, beneath the echoing cloisters pale,
    I heard of guilt and wondered at the tale!
                                    Coleridge.

39. She also had a twilight tinge of "*Blue*,"
    Could write rhymes, and compose more than she
        wrote;
  Made epigrams occasionally too
    Upon her friends, as everybody ought.
Byron.

40. I'm dull and sad! indeed, indeed,
    I know I have no reason!
  Perhaps I am not well in health,
    And 'tis a gloomy season.
Coleridge.

41. When by herself, she to herself
    Must sing some merry rhyme;
  She could not now be glad for hours,
    Yet silent all the time.
Coleridge.

42. Ye ladies, take a hint from me,
  Ne'er with the bottle make too free,
  Until you safely married be.
Old Song.

43. Would you know my chief delight?
  'Tis to enjoy a moonlight night,—
  To sit and count the stars above,
  And talk, to one that's fair, of love.
Bryant.

44. We blush, smile, or frown, as he's right or he's wrong,
  We dance when we please, or we sing him a song,
  And before we are wed, if we feel the least pique,
  We can then hold our tongues, if we like, for a week.
Bryant.

45. I never could discover
    Why listening to a lover,
      Throughout the livelong day,
    Should be miscalled offence;
    It is not common sense—
      That's all I say.

                                        Reynolds.

46. I have a silent sorrow here,
    A grief I'll ne'er impart;
    It breathes no sigh, it sheds no tear,
    But it consumes my heart.

                                        Sheridan.

47. No more by sorrow chased, my heart
    Shall yield to fell despair;
    Now joy repels the envenomed dart,
    And conquers every care.

                                        Dibdin.

48. Though deep shades delight me, yet love is my food,
    As I call the dear name of my Joe;
    His musical shout is the pride of the wood,
    And my heart leaps to hear the hallo!

                                        Bloomfield.

49. Maiden, once gay pleasure knew thee,
    Now thy cheeks are pale and deep;
    Love has been a felon to thee,
    Yet, poor maiden, do not weep.

                                      H. K. White.

50. I'll dress and I'll strut with an air,
    The barber shall frizzle my hair.

                                        O'Keefe.

What Scenery do you prefer?

———

WE look; and lo, the sea is white with sails
Innumerable, wafting to the shore
Treasures untold; the vale, the promontories,
A dream of glory; temples, palaces,
Called up as by enchantment; aqueducts
Among the groves and glades rolling along
Rivers, on many an arch high over-head;
And in the centre, like a burning sun,
The Imperial City!

Rogers.

2. Let others love the city,
    And gaudy show at sunny noon;
Gi'e me the lonely valley,
    The dewy eve, and rising moon,
Fair-beaming, and streaming,
    Her silver light the boughs amang;
While falling, recalling,
    The amorous thrush concludes her sang.

Burns.

89

3. Sweet Auburn! loveliest village of the plain,
   Where health and plenty cheered the labouring swain,
   Where smiling spring its earliest visit paid,
   And parting summer's lingering blooms delayed.

   Goldsmith.

4. His warm but simple home, where he enjoys
   With her who shares his pleasure and his heart,
   Sweet converse.

   Cowper.

5. Night on the waves! and the moon is on high,
   Hung like a gem on the brow of the sky;
   Treading its depths, in the power of her might,
   And turning the clouds, as they pass her, to light.

   Hervey.

6.   Above me are the Alps,
   The palaces of nature, whose vast walls
   Have pinnacled in clouds their snowy scalps,
   And throned eternity in icy halls
   Of cold sublimity, where forms and falls
   The avalanche—the thunderbolt of snow!
   All that expands the spirit, yet appals,
   Gather around these summits, or to show
   How earth may pierce to heaven, yet leave vain man
      below.

   Byron.

7. Brown night retires; young day pours in apace,
   And opens all the lawny prospect wide.
   The dripping rock, the mountain's misty top,
   Swell on the sight, and brighten with the dawn.

   Thomson.

8. The glorious landscape smiles and melts;
   Green wave-like meadows here are spread,
   There woodland shades are sweetly shed,
   In deepening gold there glows the wheat,
   And there the rye-field's vying sheet.
   Street.

9. Within the sunlit forest,
     Our roof the bright blue sky,
   Where streamlets flow, and wild flowers blow,
     We lift our hearts on high.
   Elliott.

10. 'Tis midnight: on the mountain's brown
    The cold, round moon shines deeply down;
    Blue roll the waters, blue the sky
    Spreads like an ocean hung on high.
    Byron.

11. The sea! the sea! the open sea!
    The blue, the fresh, the ever free!
    Without a mark, without a bound,
    It runneth the earth's wide regions round.
    Proctor.

12. Oh! a blue summer night,
      When the stars were asleep,
      Like gems of the deep,
    In their own drowsy light;
      While the new-mown hay
      On the green earth lay,
    And all that came near it went scented away.
    Neal.

13. Welcome, ye shades! ye bowery thickets, hail!
    Ye lofty pines!   Ye venerable oaks!
    Ye ashes wild, resounding o'er the steep!
    Delicious is your shelter to the soul.

                                    Thomson.

14. And leads me to the mountain-brow,
    Where sits the shepherd on the grassy turf,
    Inhaling, healthful, the descending sun,
    Around him feeds his many bleating flock,
    Of various cadence; and his sportive lambs,
    This way and that convolved, in friskful glee,
    Their frolics play.

                                    Thomson.

15. Sweet is thy coming spring! and, as I pass
    Thy hedge-rows, where from the half-naked sprays
    Peeps the sweet bud, and midst the dewy grass
    The tufted primrose opens to the day:
    My spirits light and pure confess thy power
    Of balmiest influence.

                                    Athenæum.

16. The tender Twilight with a crimson cheek
    Leans on the breast of Evening.
    How tenderly the trembling light yet plays
       On the far-waving foliage! day's last blush
    Still lingers on the billowy waste of leaves
       With a strange beauty—like the yellow flush
    That haunts the ocean when the day goes by.

                                    McLellan.

17. The evening sun's gaen down the west,
    The birds sit nodding on the tree;
    All nature now prepares for rest.
                            Tannahill.

18. Behold the hills and vales around
    With lowing herds and flocks abound;
    The wanton kids and frisking lambs
    Gambol and dance around their dams.
                            Bryce.

19. This shadowy desert, unfrequented woods,
    I better brook than flourishing peopled towns.
                            Shakspeare.

20. Above that dark, romantic stream
    Gray rocks and gloomy forests tower,
    And o'er its sullen floods the dream
    Of Lethe seems to lower;
    Low, shadowed by its frowning steeps,
    The deep and turbid river sweeps.
                            Sisters of the West.

21. Within a southern garden, where the breath
    Of flowers went up like incense, and the plash
    Of falling fountains made a murmuring voice
    Of music sweet, yet same.
                            Sisters of the West.

22. Where the pale flowers grow rank and wild,
    In that sequestered solitude,
    Where never hath the sunshine smiled,
    And step may not intrude.
                            Sisters of the West.

23. Twilight's soft dews steal o'er the village-green,
With magic tints to harmonize the scene.
Stilled is the hum that through the hamlet broke,
When round the ruins of their ancient oak
The peasants flocked to hear the minstrel play,
And games and carols closed the busy day.
                                        Rogers.

24. The festival was high and proud,
    The lamps were dazzling clear;
And pealing music, long and loud,
    Rushed on the listening ear.
                            Sisters of the West.

25. In those primeval forests, oh! did the red deer bound,
    Tossing their dark-brown antlers—trampling the
        new-made ground?
    And did the huge bald eagle over thy waters brood?
    Or didst thou, now-born giant, track one vast solitude?
                            Sisters of the West.

26.   Oh! let me go abroad
Into the breast of nature; where the wind
    Makes solemn music in the forest tree;
Swaying the old, gray, twisting vines, that bind
    Branch unto branch with its wild minstrelsy.
                            Sisters of the West.

27. We stand upon a breezy hill
    That overhangs the deep;
Beneath our feet the scant grass springs,
    Above us eagles sweep.
                            Sisters of the West.

28. I stood on the lone forest side.   I viewed
      The wild luxuriant blossoms at my feet;
    I saw around me stretch the giant wood;
      I watched the swift deer, bounding wild and fleet.
                                 Sisters of the West.

29. When o'er the waves the lightnings flash,
      And many a gallant bark is riven;
    And solemnly the thunder's crash
      Peals from the darkened face of heaven!
                                 Sisters of the West.

30. And oh! the time of winter, when round the hearth
        by night
    We sat, glad little children, by the broad red fire
        light;
    Wild and stormy stories to hear with young amaze.
                                 Sisters of the West.

31. Where the moonbeam flieth
      O'er the lone sea,
    There a sweet voice crieth,
      I wait for thee!
                                 Sisters of the West.

32. I watch their deep and household joy,
      Around the evening hearth;
    When the children stand beside each knee,
      With laugh and shout of mirth.
                                 Sisters of the West.

33. The crowded mart, the lofty hall,
      The palace and the bower.
                                 Sisters of the West.

34. Where the first violets their fragrance shed;
Where the old oak trees wore the earliest green,
And the moss crept in love, around the brim
Of that old fountain, ruined but not dim.
                                        Sisters of the West.

35. I have stood in caverns, where never came
A ray of light, save the torches' flame,
As they gleamed on the walls with their glittering
        spars,
And the arching roof with its mimic stars.
                                        Sisters of the West.

36. Say that when evening shades
    Fall over land and lea,
I'll stand beneath those green arcades,
    Where once we wandered free.
                                        Sisters of the West.

37. And the pale stars, their evening rays are streaming
    On the still water, through the shadowy trees;
Then, in the sadness of thy mystic dreaming,
    My spirit's power shall mingle even with these.
                                        Sisters of the West.

38. Lead me beneath the locust trees,
    Where grass and violets spring,
And whence the gentle summer breeze
    Bears fragrance on its wing.
                                        Sisters of the West.

39. I know these ruins gray,
    I know these cloisters dim—
My soul hath been in these walls away,
    When slumber chains each limb.
Sisters of the West.

40. To seek the mountain side, and forest glade,
Or the transparent lake, whose waters wear
The glorious semblance of the sunset heaven.
Sisters of the West.

41. That scene, that rushing river,
    That forest, lone and dim,
Where the winds made a low shiver
    Like the echo of a hymn.
Sisters of the West.

42. And 'neath the tall magnolias, and each grove
Of laurel, where the native shrines had place
Amid the myrtle boughs, that breathed of love.
Sisters of the West.

43. The forms of silent, threatening hosts,
Amid them waving pennons and standards proud;
And white walled tents and gay pavilions gleam,
Of cloth of gold, hung o'er with burnished arms
That flicker in the sunlight.
Boker.

44. Nature's young, giddy scions shout,
    Birds scream from out the dancing trees;
The blue-eyed violets wink about,
    And toss their odours on the breeze.
Boker.

7

45. The rough north whitens the softening land,
    And binds the plains and streams in winter's
        numbing band.
    Now on the smoking ground falls spring-like rain,
    And hub deep sinks the rocking, labouring wain.

                                    Boker.

46. Thickest night, o'erhang my dwelling!
        Howling tempest, o'er me rave!
    Turbid torrents, wintry swelling,
        Still surround my lonely cave!

                                    Burns.

47. The forests are leafless, the meadows are brown,
    And all the gay foppery of summer is flown;
    Apart let me wander, apart let me muse.

                                    Burns.

48. Flow gently, sweet Afton, among thy green braes,
    Flow gently, I'll sing thee a song in thy praise.

                                    Burns.

49. As I stood by yon roofless tower,
        Where the wall-flower scents the dewy air,
    Where the howlet mourns in her ivy bower,
        And the midnight moon her care.

                                    Burns.

50. Among the heathy hills and ragged woods,
    The roaring Fyers pours his mossy floods;
    Till full he dashes on the rocky mounds,
    Where, through a shapeless breach, his stream
        resounds.

                                    Burns.

𝔚𝔥𝔞𝔱 𝔦𝔰 𝔶𝔬𝔲𝔯 𝔚𝔬𝔯𝔩𝔡𝔩𝔶 ℭ𝔬𝔫𝔡𝔦𝔱𝔦𝔬𝔫?

 HAVE five hundred crowns,
The thrifty hire I saved under your father,
Which I did store, to be my foster nurse,
When service should in my old limbs lie lame.
Shakspeare.

2. Can wealth give happiness? Look round, and see
What gay distress! what splendid misery!
Whatever fortune lavishly can pour,
The mind annihilates, and calls for more.
Young.

3. Were 't possible that wit could turn a penny,
Poets might then grow rich as well as any:
For 'tis not wit to have a great estate,
The blind effect of fortune and of fate.
Buckingham.

4. My riches a's my penny fee,
    And I maun guide it cannie, O;
But warl's gear ne'er troubles me,
    My thoughts are a' my Nannie, O.

Burns.

5. O the weary siller!
O the weary siller!
Wha wad venture till her,
That hadna got the siller?

Q. K.

6. I'm now a gude farmer, I've acres o' land,
    An' my heart aye loups light when I'm viewin' o't,
An' I ha'e servants at my command,
    An' twa dainty cowts for the plowin' o't.
My farm is a snug ane, lies high on a muir,
The muir-cocks an' plivers aft skirl at my door,
An' whan the sky lowrs I'm aye sure o' a shower.
    To moisten my land for the plowin' o't.

A. Scott.

7. It's I ha'e seven braw new gouns,
    And ither seven better to mak';
And yet, for a' my new gouns,
    My wooer has turned his back.
Besides, I have seven milk-kye,
    And Sandy he has but three;
And yet, for a' my gude kye,
    The laddie winna ha'e me.

Ramsay.

8 My father has baith gowd and gear,
    Forby a bonnie maiden free:
    My mither spins wi' eident care,
      An' daughters they ha'e nane but me.
    But what care I for gowd and gear,
      Or what care I for maidens free;
    I wadna gi'e a bonnie lad
      For a' the gowd in Chrisendie.
                           Paul.

9. An empty purse is ill to wear,
     An empty purse is ill to share.
                           Anon.

10. I ha'e gowd and gear; I ha'e land eneuch;
     I ha'e seven good oxen gangin' in a pleuch.
                         Old Song.

11. I ha'e a gude ha' house, a barn, and a byre,
     A stack afore the door; I'll mak' a rantin fire:
     I'll mak' a rantin fire, and merry shall we be:
     And, gin ye winna tak' me, I can let ye be.
                         Old Song.

12. Behind the door a bag of meal,
     And in the kist was plenty
    Of good hard cakes his mither bakes,
     And bannocks were na scanty;
    A good fat sow, a sleeky cow
     Was standin' in the byre;
    Whilst lazy pouss with mealy mou's
     Was playing at the fire.
                         Clerk.

13. Has aye a penny in his purse
    For dinner and for supper;
And if ye please, a good fat cheese,
    And lumps of yellow butter.
                                Clerk.

14. We loo'd the liquor well enough;
    But waes my heart my cash was done,
Before that I had quenched my drouth,
    And laith I was to pawn my shoon.
                                Ramsay.

15. I ance had a weel theekit cot-house
    On Morvala's sea-beaten shore;
But our laird turned me out frae my cot-house;
    Alas! I was feckless an' puir.
                                Burns.

16. See ye not yon hills and dales,
    The sun shines on sae brawlie!
They a' are mine, and they shall be thine.
                                Anon.

17. Whan I'd nae need o' aid, there were plenty to proffer;
And noo whan I want it, I ne'er get the offer:
I could grieve whan I think hoo my siller decreast,
In the feasting o' those wha came only to feast.
                                Anderson.

18. What though on hamely fare we dine,
    Wear hoddin-gray, and a' that?
Gi'e the fools their silks, and knaves their wine;
    A man's a man, for a' that.
                                Burns.

19. I ha'e a green purse and a wee pickle gowd,
    A bonnie piece lan' an' a plantin' on't,
It fattens my flocks, an' my barns it has stowed,
    But the best thing o' a's yet a-wantin' on't.
                    Anon.

20. I was once a weel-tochered lass,
    My mither left dollars to me,
But now I'm brought to a poor pass,
    My step-dame has gart them flee.
                    Ramsay.

21. I've baith bread and kitchen nae scanty,
    An' gowns i' the fashion fu' braw:
But aye there's an unco bit wantie,
    That fashes me mair than them a'.
                    Watson.

22. He left me wi' his deein' breath
    A dwallin' house, an' a' that;
A barn, a byre, an' wabs o' claith—
    A big peat-stack, an a' that.
    A mare, a foal, an a' that,
    A mare, a foal, an a' that,
Sax guid fat kye, a cauf forby,
    An' twa pet ewes, an' a' that.
                    Somerville.

23. And though our fortune is but low,
    Though we have yet but little store,
I'll wield the spade, and ply the hoe,
    And strive to make that little more.
                    Hunter.

24. Wi' sma' to sell, and less to buy,
    Abeen distress, below envy,
    O wha wad leave this humble state,
    For a' the pride of a' the great?

Burns.

25. When I think on this world's pelf,
    And the little wee share I ha'e o't to myself,
    And how the lass that wants it is by the lads forgot,
    May the shame fa' the gear and the blaithrie o't!

Anon.

26. An' you sall wear, when you are wed,
    The kirtle an' the Heeland plaid,
    An' sleep upon a heather bed,
      Sae cozy an' sae canty.

Shepherd.

27. There's palace-like mansions at which ye may stare,
    Where Luxury rolls in her soft easy-chair,—
    At least puir folks think sae,—their knowledge is
      sma',
    There's far more contentment at Sandyford ha'.
    There's something romantic about an auld house,
    Where the cock ilka morning keeps crawling fu'
      crouse,
    An' the kye in the byre are baith sleekit an' braw,
    An' such is the case at blithe Sandyford ha'.

Park.

28. Fortune and I are friends.

Shakspeare.

29. A woman impudent and mannish grown
  Is not more loathed than an effeminate man
  In time of action.
  Shakspeare.

30. A fane forsaken, and a hearth deserted—
  A prison tenantless, and void, and dim,
  Whence the acquitted have in joy departed—
  These are the relics that remain to him.
  Sisters of the West.

31. Nor ope her lap to saint-seducing gold:
  Oh, she is rich in beauty; only poor,
  That, when she dies, with beauty dies her store.
  Shakspeare.

32. Although a lad were o'er so smart,
  If that he wants the yellow dirt,
  You'll cast your head another airt,
  And answer him full dry.
  Burns.

33. How shall your houseless heads and unfed sides,
  Your looped and windowed raggedness, defend you
  From seasons such as these.
  Shakspeare.

34. A coach, with six footmen behind,
  I count neither trifle nor sin;
  But, ye gods, how oft do we find
  A scandalous trifle within?
  Farquhar.

·35. I am a tailor gay
     As ever wore a thimble,
Through life I work away,
     My fingers always nimble;
Although threadbare of wit,
     The lasses I can wheedle.

                  Dibdin.

36. I've buckles—silver, gold, and brass,
     And shoes, to trip with grace in;
Sashes, ribbons, laces strong, for those who've need
         to lace in.

                  McFarren.

37. What now remains were easy told,
Tom comes, his pockets lined with gold,
Now rich enough, no more to roam.

                  Dibdin.

38. A gentleman so rich in the world's goods,
Handsome and young, enjoying all the present.

                  Byron.

39. Why call the miser miserable? as
I said before: the frugal life is his,
Which in a saint or cynic ever was
The theme of praise.

                  Byron.

40. Young Ben he was a nice young man,
A carpenter by trade.

                  Old Song.

41. Where's he for honest poverty
    That hangs his head and a' that?
    The coward slave, we pass him by,
    And dare be poor for a' that!
                                    Burns.

42. Then she's got a fine stock of clothes,
    With her grandmother's holiday hose,
    Made out of the very best yarn,
    Full of holes, but never a darn.
                                    Hickman.

43. Can wealth or friends thy heart incline
    To scorn my humble lot?
                                    Old Song.

44. With a rich pair of pockets o'erflowing with charms.
                                    Dibdin.

45. Wealth and power, what are ye worth,
    To pleasure if you give not birth?
    Rich in ambition's gilded toys,
    I barter them for real joys.
                                    Cobb.

46. To poverty we'll bid adieu,
      My heart with joy abounds;
    Lord! what a deal we all may do
      With ten thousand pounds.
                                    Romer.

47. I ask not wealth, I ask not power,
      Content must ever be
    Where'er thou dwell'st, and every hour
      Be bliss that's shared with thee.
                                    Baylies.

48. I'll buy ye new silks and fine satins to wear,
       You'll dress yourself up every day like a lady
         bright;
      Sit yourself down in my mother's great chair,
       And scold all the servants from morning till night.
                              Hudson.

49. Though others may boast of more riches than mine,
       And rate my attractions e'en fewer,
      At their jeers and attractions I'll scorn to repine,
       Can they boast of a heart that is truer?
                           English Song.

50. In this mighty city how easy to live,
       For credit's the soul of the place;
      Which great and small equally give and receive,
       So credit can be no disgrace.
                           Dibdin.

Describe your Future Residence.

INE be a cot beside the hill;
   A bee-hive's hum shall soothe my ear;
   A willowy brook that turns a mill,
   With many a fall shall linger near.

Rogers.

2. My eyes make pictures when they're shut:—
   I see a fountain large and fair,
A willow and a ruined hut,
   And thee and me and Mary there.
O Mary! make thy gentle lap our pillow;
Bend o'er us like a bower, my beautiful green willow.

Coleridge.

3. Whoe'er has travelled life's dull round,
   Where'er his stages may have been,
May sigh to think he still has found
   The warmest welcome at an inn.

Shenstone.

4. Oh! ask not a home in the mansions of pride,
    Where marble shines out in the pillars and walls;
Though the roof be of gold, it is brilliantly cold,
    And joy may not be found in its torch-lighted halls.
                                Eliza Cook.

5. Oh for a lodge in some vast wilderness,
    Some boundless contiguity of shade.
                                Cowper.

6.   Halfway up
    He built his house, whence by stealth he caught,
    Among the hills, a glimpse of busy life,
    That soothed, not stirred.
                                Rogers.

7. Oh haste, unfold the hospitable hall!
    That hall, where once, in antiquated state,
    The chair of justice held the grave debate.
                                Rogers.

8. My Highland home, where tempests blow,
        And cold thy wintry looks,
    Thy mountains crowned with driven snow,
        And ice-bound are thy brooks!
                                Morton.

9. Go make thy home
        In some desert place,
    Which no voice may gladden,
        No footsteps grace.
                                Sisters of the West.

10. Some cottage-home, from towns and toil remote,
    Where love and lore may calm alternate hours.
                              Campbell.

11. No home! no home! Oh, weary one!
    And art thou like the dove of yore,
    Who found no spot to rest upon,
    Wandering the waste of waters o'er?
                    Sisters of the West.

12. And thou art like that God-struck man,
    Forever wandering on;
    Thy spirit's doom is weird and wan;
    Alone! alone! alone!
                    Sisters of the West.

13.   I could be happy there!
    In that low cot embowered in deepest shade,
    And lying in a lone and lovely glade.
                    Sisters of the West.

14. At length his lonely cot appears in view,
    Beneath the shelter of an aged tree.
                    Burns.

15. I knew by the smoke, that so gracefully curled
    Above the green elms, that a cottage was near;
    And I said, If there's peace to be found in the world,
    A heart that is humble might hope for it here.
                    Moore.

16. To lie in kilns and barns at e'en,
    When bones are crazed and blood is thin,
    Is doubtless great distress.
                    Burns.

17. Very near the west end, though I must not tell
      where.

                                            L. W. K.

18.   It is a hall
  Where people dance, and sup, and dance again.
                                            Byron.

19. Into one of the sweetest of hotels,
      Especially for foreigners—and mostly
  For those whom favour or whom fortune swells,
      And cannot find a bill's small items costly.
                                            Byron.

20. The mansion's self was vast and venerable,
      With more of the monastic than has been
  Elsewhere preserved: the cloisters still were stable,
      The cells too and refectory, I ween.
                                            Byron.

21. Low was our pretty cot: our tallest rose
  Peeped at the chamber-window. We could hear,
  At silent noon, and eve, and early morn,
  The sea's faint murmur.
                                            Coleridge.

22. A beautiful garden with weeds overrun,
  And an elegant fish-pond dried up by the sun;
  Then the house stood convenient enough, you may
      say,
  Next door to the whisky-shop over the way.
                                            Dibdin.

23. A green and silent spot, amid the hills,
   A small and silent dell!   O'er stiller place
   No sinking sky-lark ever poised himself.
                                         Coleridge.

24. My house in Duke's Place is
   The mart of the Graces,
   Vat show their sweet faces
      By light of the lamps.
                                         Box.

25. I will twine thee a bower,
      By the clear siller fountain,
   And I'll cover it o'er
      Wi' the flowers of the mountain;
   I will range through the wilds,
      And the deep glens sae dreary,
   And return wi' the spoils
      To the bower o' my dearie.
                                         Tannahill.

26. Here naught but Candour reigns, indulgent Ease,
      Good-nature lounging, sauntering up and down:
   They who are pleased themselves must always please;
      On others' ways they never squint a frown.
                                         Thomson.

27. The rooms with costly tapestry were hung,
      Where was inwoven many a gentle tale,
   Such as of old the rural poets sung,
      Or of Arcadian or Sicilian vale.
                                         Thomson.

8

28. My house a cottage, more
    Than palace, and should fitting be
    For all my use, no luxury.
                            Cowley.

29. Then, too, the pillared dome, magnific, heaved
    Its ample roof; and Luxury within
    Poured out her glittering stores.
                          Thomson.

30. Here wealth still swells the golden tide,
      As busy trade his labour plies;
    There architecture's noble pride
      Bids elegance and splendour rise.
                          Burns.

31. Mid piles beneath whose fretted cornices
    Echo still babbles of a glorious past.
                         Edith May.

32. Above, bright glimpses of the purest blue;
      Around, the fir trees' sombre depth of shade,
    Save where some sapling of a brighter hue
      Starts from the covert as if half afraid.
                  Elizabeth Emmet.

33. There is not in the wide world a valley so sweet
    As that vale in whose bosom the bright waters meet;
    Oh! the last rays of feeling and life must depart,
    Ere the bloom of that valley shall fade from my
        heart.
                          Moore.

34. Yes! thou art changed, my mountain home;
    Yet still my heart doth cling to thee,
The spot where I was wont to roam,
From grief and sadness free.
                              W. G. H.

35. Fountains leaping, vinelets creeping,
    Mark where she moves;
Tendrils clinging, sweet birds singing,
    Tell how she loves.
                              H. F. Gould.

36. Where a lone castle by the sea
    Upreared its dark and mouldering pile,
Far seen, with all its frowning towers,
For many and many a weary mile.
               Anna M. Power and Sarah H. Whitman.

37. 'Twas an humble, moss-grown cot,
    Where the maid of the sun-bright hair
Dwelt with a crone who loved her not:
She was wrinkled and old with care.
                              Kate St. Clair.

38. The ruddy hearth-fires gleam and fade
    Upon the dusky wall,
And on the darkened ceiling
    Fantastic shadows fall;
No sound is heard in all the house,
    So lonely now and drear,
And e'en the cricket's drowsy song
    Falls faintly on her ear.
               Anna M. Power and Sarah H. Whitman.

39. And he lived "up town," in a splendid square,
    And kept his daughter on dainty fare,
    And gave her gems that were rich and rare,
    And the finest rings and things to wear,
      And feathers enough to plume her!
                    J. G. Saxe.

40. 'Twas a dreadful change in human affairs,
    From a place "Up Town" to a nook "Up Stairs,"
      From an avenue down to an alley!
                    J. G. Saxe.

41. A lordly oak, with spreading arms,
    By my mountain-dwelling grew.
    O'er the roof and chimney-top
      Uprose that glorious tree;
    No giant of all the forests round
      Had mightier boughs than he.
                    J. H. Bryant.

42. So what I but guessed, my Mabel,
      The bird hath told at will,
    That you're going to marry the miller,
      And live beside the mill.
                Mrs. M. N. McDonald.

43. On marble stairs, and tessellated hall,
    Scarce heard was her retiring footstep-fall,
      While passing to her trocador,
    Where, while she bathed, Arabian maids shampooed
    Their royal mistress; and perfume renewed
      Through perforated chamber floor.
                    Anon.

44. There's a homestead of beauty by Delaware's stream,
    And the sweet tones of children are ringing all day,
  While the voice of the mother is blithesome and glad,
    As the notes of the song-bird that warbles in May.
  The angel of peace to the hearth-stone has come,
    With a message of mercy to brighten each dream,
  And as glad to the heart, as 'tis pure to the eye,
    Is that homestead of beauty by Delaware's stream.
                              S. D. Anderson.

45. Land of poets, Italy,
    As the rivers seek the sea,
    Floats my dreaming soul to thee.
                              O. Allen.

46. Round our old paternal dwelling
    Here, 'tis all a hush profound,
    Save an infant zephyr swelling,
    'Tis to memory spirit-ground.
                              H. F. Gould.

47. Our father lives in Washington,
    And has a world of cares,
    But gives his children each a farm,
    Enough for them and theirs.
                              Mrs. L. H. Sigourney.

48. But where the rivulet runneth
    In the bottom of the glen.
                              K. R. M.

49. A city mansion, neat, nor proud,
    Where Business hums his song aloud.
                              C. Watson.

Missing Page

Missing Page

4. And now old Murmur all alone
   Has none to close the Grumbler's eyes.

Cherry.

5. It is that settled ceaseless gloom
   The fabled Hebrew wanderer bore,
That will not look beyond the tomb,
But cannot hope for rest before.

Byron.

6. Ambition holds the nectared drink,
   It in the golden vase looks fair;
But what fond lip can touch the brink
Nor quaff a sea of sorrows there?

Kelly.

7. For soon the winter of the year,
And age, life's winter, will appear;
At this, thy lovely bloom will fade,
As that will strip the verdant shade.

Mallet.

8. Yet pilot-honour shall not fail
To weather every dangerous gale;
And, to old age as we subside,
Delight our smiling fire-side.

Dibdin.

9. The sight which keen affection clears,
   How can it judge amiss?
To me it pictured hope, and taught
My spirit this consoling thought,—
That Love's sun, though it rise in tears,
   May set in bliss.

Strangford.

10. Calm to peace thy lover's bosom—
　　Can it, dearest, must it be?
　　Thou within an hour shalt lose him,
　　He forever loses thee!
　　　　　　　　　　　　　　Moore.

11. If but little your own you can call,
　　It's quite certain much you cannot pay;
　　And if you've got nothing at all,
　　Why, you're sure they can't take it away.
　　　　　　　　　　　　　Old Song.

12. Toil only gives the soul to shine,
　　And makes rest fragrant and benign;
　　A heritage, it seems to me,
　　Worth being poor to hold in fee.
　　　　　　　　　　　　J. R. Lowell.

13. When fortune raiseth to the greatest height,
　　The happy man should most suppress his state;
　　Expecting still a change of things to find,
　　And fearing when the gods appear too kind.
　　　　　　　　　　　　R. Howard.

14. Prosperity puts out unnumbered thoughts,
　　Of import high, and light divine, to man.
　　　　　　　　　　　　　Young.

15. How beautiful is sorrow, when 'tis drest
　　By virgin innocence! It makes
　　Felicity in others seem deformed.
　　　　　　　　　　　　W. Davenant.

16. Our wedding cheer to a sad burial feast;
    Our solemn hymns to sullen dirges change;
    Our bridal flowers serve for a buried corse,
    And all things change them to the contrary.
    Shakspeare.

17. Oh! ever thus from childhood's hour
        I've seen my fondest hopes decay;
    I never loved a tree or flower,
        But 'twas the first to fade away.
    Moore.

18.   There comes
    For ever something between us and what
    We deem our happiness.
    Byron.

19. And therefore—since I cannot prove a lover,
    To entertain these fair well-spoken days—
    I am determined to prove a villain,
    And hate the idle pleasures of these days.
    Shakspeare.

20. Whoever, with an earnest soul,
        Strives for some end from this low world afar,
    Still upward travels though he miss the goal,
        And strays—but towards a star!
    Bulwer.

21. These base mechanics never keep their words
    In any thing they promise. 'Tis their trade
    To swear and break; they all grow rich by breaking
    More than their words.
    Jonson.

22. I dwell amid the city,
    And hear the flow of souls!
                              Miss Barrett.

23. Though at times my spirit fails me,
    And the bitter tear-drops fall,
    Though my lot is hard and lonely,
    Yet I hope—I hope through all.
                              Mrs. Norton.

24. Shortly his fortune shall be lifted higher;
    True industry doth kindle honour's fire.
                              Shakspeare.

25. How blest the farmer's simple life!
    How pure the joy it yields!
    Far from the world's tempestuous strife,
    Free mid the scented fields!
                              C. W. Everest.

·26.   Walk
    Boldly and wisely in that light thou hast;—
    There is a hand above will help thee on.
                              Bailey.

27. Let error act, opinion speak,
    And want afflict, and sickness break,
    And anger burn, dejection chill,
    And joy distract, and sorrow kill,
    Till, armed by care, and taught to mow,
    Time draws the long destructive blow.
                              Parnell.

28. Unrivalled as thy merit, be thy fame.
                              Tickell.

29. But midst the crowd, the hum, the shock of men,
　　　To hear, to see, to feel, and to possess,
　　And roam along, the world's tired denizen,
　　　With none who bless us, none whom we may bless.
　　　　　　　　　　　　　　　　Byron.

30. Now I recentre my immortal mind
　　In the deep Sabbath of meek self-content;
　　Cleansed from the vaporous passions that bedim
　　God's image.
　　　　　　　　　　　　　　Coleridge.

31. The seals of office glitter in his eyes;
　　He climbs, he pants, he grasps them; at his heels,
　　Close at his heels, a demagogue ascends,
　　And with a dexterous jerk soon twists him down,
　　And wins them, but to lose them in his turn.
　　　　　　　　　　　　　　　Cowper.

32. Fathers their children and themselves abuse,
　　That wealth, a husband for their daughters choose.
　　　　　　　　　　　　　　　Shirley.

33. Me let the tender office long engage
　　To rock the cradle of reposing age;
　　With lenient arts extend a mother's breath,
　　Make languor smile, and smooth the bed of death.
　　　　　　　　　　　　　　　　Pope.

34. I fly like a bird of the air,
　　　In search of a home and a rest;
　　A balm for the sickness of care;
　　　A bliss for a bosom unblest.
　　　　　　　　　　　　　　　Byron.

35. Here's a sigh to those who love me,
And a smile to those who hate;
And, whatever sky's above me,
Here's a heart for every fate.

Byron.

36. There are two hearts whose movements thrill
In unison so closely sweet!
That pulse to pulse responsive still,
They both must heave—or cease to beat.

B. Barton.

37. His life is calm and blessed, for his peace,
Like a rich pearl beyond the diver's ken,
Lies deep in his own bosom. He is pure,
For the soul's errands are not done with men;
His senses are subdued and serve the soul.

Willis.

38. —Forced to drudge for the dregs of men,
And scrawl strange words with the barbarous pen,
And mingle among the jostling crowd,
Where the sons of strife are busy and loud.

Bryant.

39. For foreign glory, foreign joy, they roam;
No thought of peace or happiness at home.
But wisdom's triumph is well timed retreat,
As hard a science to the fair as great!

Pope.

40. Oh happiness of sweet retired content!
To be at once secure and innocent.

Denham.

41.   Famine is in thy cheeks,
   Need and oppression stareth in thine eyes,
   Upon thy back hangs ragged misery,
   The world is not thy friend, nor the world's law.
                                   Shakspeare.

42. Though the lamp of his fame will continue to burn,
   When even his dust to the dust shall return,
   And for ages to come a bright halo will throw
   O'er the mouldering remains of the mighty Munro.
                                   Finlay.

43. How miserable a thing is a great man:
   Take noisy vexing greatness they that please,
   Give me obscure, and safe, and silent ease.
                                   Crown.

44. The rich man's son inherits lands,
      And piles of brick, and stone, and gold,
   And he inherits soft white hands,
      And tender flesh that fears the cold,
      Nor dares to wear a garment old.
                                   J. R. Lowell.

45. May dool and sorrow be his chance,
   Dool and sorrow, dool and sorrow,
   May dool and sorrow be his chance,
      And nane say, Wae's me for 'im!
                                   Skinner.

46. Virtue is choked with foul ambition,
      And charity chased hence by rancour's hand;
   Foul subornation is predominant.
                                   Shakspeare.

47. He's comin' frae the North that's to fancy me,
   He's comin' frae the North that's to fancy me;
   A feather in his bonnet and a ribbon at his knee,
   He's a bonnie, bonnie laddie, an yon be he.

   Burns.

48. Sigh no more, lady, sigh no more,
   　Men were deceivers ever;
   One foot in sea, and one on shore;
   　To one thing constant never.

   Shakspeare.

49. They that stand high have many blasts to shake
   　them;
   And, if they fall, they dash themselves to pieces.

   Shakspeare.

50.　　　　　Truth shall nurse her,
   Holy and heavenly thoughts still counsel her:
   She shall be loved, and feared: her own shall bless
   　her,
   Her foes shake like a field of beaten corn,
   And hang their heads with sorrow: good grows with
   　her.

   Shakspeare.

What Music do you love?

WHERE Claribel low-lieth
The breezes pause and die,
Letting the rose leaves fall:
But the solemn oak-tree sigheth,
Thick-leaved, ambrosial,
With an ancient melody
Of an inward agony,
Where Claribel low lieth.
At eve the beetle boometh
Athwart the thicket lone:
At noon the bee low hummeth
About the mossed headstone:
At midnight the moon cometh,
And looketh down alone.
Her song the lintwhite swelleth
The clear-voiced mavis dwelleth,
The fledging throstle lispeth,
The slumbrous wave outwelleth,
The babbling runnel crispeth,
The hollow grot replieth
Where Claribel low lieth.

Tennyson.

2. I heard no sounds, but such as evening sends
   Up from the city to these quiet shades;
   A blended murmur sweetly harmonizing
   With flowing fountains, feathered minstrelsy,
   And voices from the hills.
   Hillhouse.

3. So evening's charming voices, welcomed ever,
   As signs of rest and peace;—the watchman's call,
   The closing gates, the Levite's mellow trump
   Announcing the returning moon, the pipe
   Of swains, the bleat, the bark, the housing-bell.
   Hillhouse.

4. What wakest thou, Spring?—sweet voices in the
           woods,
      And reed-like echoes, that have long been mute;
   Thou bringest back, to fill the solitudes,
      The lark's clear pipe, the cuckoo's viewless flute,
   Whose tone seems breathing mournfulness or glee,
           Even as our hearts may be.
   Hemans.

5. By the sleepy ripple of the stream,
   Which hath lulled thee into many a dream;
   By the shiver of the ivy-leaves
   To the wind of morn at thy casement-eaves,
   By the bees' deep murmur in the limes,
   By the music of the Sabbath-chimes,   -
   By every sound of thy native shade,
   Stronger and dearer the spell is made.
   Hemans.

6. The sparrow's chirrup on the roof,
    The slow clock ticking, and the sound
Which to the wooing wind aloof
    The poplar made.
                                    Tennyson.

7.   Sometimes, when I'm alone,
Just ere his coming, I have heard a sound,
A strange, mysterious, melancholy sound,
Like music in the air.   Like wild sad music,
More moving than the lute or viol touched
By skilful fingers.   Wailing in the air
It seems around me, and withdraws as when
One looks and lingers for a last adieu.
                                    Hillhouse.

8. Thou hast been o'er solitary seas, and from their
        wastes brought back
    Each noise of waters that awoke in the mystery of
        thy track;
    The chime of low soft southern waves on some green
        palmy shore,
    The hollow roll of distant surge, the gathered billow's
        roar.
                                    Hemans.

9. The lintwhite and the throstlecock
    Have voices sweet and clear;
        All in the blooméd May.
    They from the blosmy brere
    Call to the fleeting year,
    If that he would them hear
        And stay.
                                    Tennyson.

10. The jar of life is still; the city speaks
In gentle murmurs· voices chime with lutes
Waked in the streets and gardens; loving pairs
Eye the red west in one another's arms;
And nature, breathing dew and fragrance, yields
A glimpse of happiness, which He, who formed
Earth and the stars, had power to make eternal.
                                    Hillhouse.

11. But thou art swelling on, thou deep,
    Through many an olden clime,
  Thy billowy anthem, ne'er to sleep
    Until the close of time.
  Thou liftest up thy solemn voice
    To every wind and sky,
  And all our earth's green shores rejoice
    In that one harmony.
  It fills the noontide's calm profound,
    The sunset's heaven of gold;
  And the still midnight hears the sound,
    E'en as when first it rolled.
  Let there be silence deep and strange,
    Where sceptred cities rose!
  Thou speak'st of one who doth not change—
    So may our hearts repose.
                                    Hemans.

12. A breeze that roves o'er stream and hill,
    Telling of winter gone,
  Hath such sweet falls—yet caught we still
    A farewell in its tone.
                                    Hemans.

13. The wild swan's death-hymn took the soul
    Of that waste place with joy
    Hidden in sorrow: at first to the ear
    The warble was low, and full and clear;
    And floating about the undersky,
    Prevailing in weakness, the coronach stole
    Sometimes afar, and sometimes anear;
    But anon her awful jubilant voice,
    With a music strange and manifold,
    Flowed forth on a carol free and bold:
    As when a mighty people rejoice
    With shawms, and with cymbals, and harps of gold,
    And the tumult of their acclaim is rolled
    Through the open gates of the city afar,
    To the shepherd who watcheth the evening star.
                                    Tennyson.

14. Then rose a nation's sound—
    Oh! what a power to bid the quick heart bound
    The wind bears onward with the stormy cheer
    Men give to glory on her high career!
    Is there indeed such power?—far deeper dwells
    In one kind household voice, to reach the cells
    Whence happiness flows forth!
                                    Hemans.

15. Ye are from dingle and fresh glade, ye flowers!
      By some kind hand to cheer my dungeon sent;
    O'er you the oak shed down the summer showers,
      And the lark's nest was where your bright cups
          bent,
    Quivering to breeze and rain-drop, like the sheen
    Of twilight stars.   On you Heaven's eye hath been.

Through the leaves, pouring its dark sultry blue
Into your glowing hearts; the bee to you
Hath murmured, and the rill.   My soul grows faint
With passionate yearning, as its quick dreams paint
Your haunts by dell and stream,—the green, the
     free,
The full of all sweet sound,—the shut from me!
                                   Hemans.

16. Then on the silence of the snows there lay
A Sabbath's quiet sunshine,—and its bell
Filled the hushed air awhile, with lonely sway;
For the stream's voice was chained by Winter's
     spell
The deep wood-sounds had ceased.   But rock and
     dell
Rung forth, ere long, when strains of jubilee
Pealed from the mountain-churches, with a swell
Of praise to Him who stills the raging sea.
                                   Hemans.

17. Heard melodies are sweet, but those unheard
     Are sweeter; therefore, ye soft pipes, play on;
Not to the sensual ear, but, more endeared,
     Pipe to the spirit ditties of no tone:
Fair youth, beneath the trees, thou canst not leave
Thy song, nor ever can those trees be bare;
     Bold Lover, never, never canst thou kiss,
Though winning near the goal—yet, do not grieve;
She cannot fade, though thou hast not thy bliss,
     For ever wilt thou love, and she be fair!
                                   Keats.

18. There came enchantment with the shifting wind,
    That did both drown and keep alive my ears.
    I threw my shell away upon the sand,
    And a wave filled it, as my sense was filled
    With that new blissful golden melody.
    A living death was in each gush of sounds,
    Each family of rapturous hurried notes,
    That fell, one after one, yet all at once,
    Like pearl beads dropping sudden from their string:
    And then another, then another strain,
    Each like a dove leaving its olive perch,
    With music winged instead of silent plumes,
    To hover round my head, and make me sick
    Of joy and grief at once.
                         Keats.

19. Awakening up, he took her hollow lute,—
    Tumultuous,—and, in chords that tenderest be,
    He played an ancient ditty, long since mute,
    In Provence called, "La belle dame sans mercy;"
    Close to her ear touching the melody;—
    Wherewith disturbed, she uttered a soft moan:
    He ceased—she panted quick—and suddenly
    Her blue affrayed eyes wide open shone:
    Upon his knees he sank, pale as smooth-sculptured
        stone.
                         Keats.

20. Only overhead the sweet nightingale
    Ever sang more sweet as the day might fail,
    And snatches of its Elysian chant
    Were mixed with the dreams of the Sensitive Plant.
                         Shelley.

21. The whirlwind is rolling,
    The thunder is tolling,
    The forest is swinging,
    The minster-bells ringing—
      Come away!
                 Shelley.

22. Like a poet hidden
     In the light of thought,
    Singing hymns unbidden,
     Till the world is wrought
    To sympathy with hopes and fears it heeded not:
    Like a high-born maiden
     In a palace tower,
    Soothing her love-laden
     Soul in secret hour
    With music sweet as love, which overflows her
      bower.
                 Shelley.

23. I stood within the city disinterred;
    And heard the autumnal leaves like light foot-
      falls
    Of spirits passing through the streets; and heard
    The Mountain's slumberous voice at intervals
    Thrill through those roofless halls;
    The oracular thunder penetrating shook
    The listening soul in my suspended blood;
    I felt that Earth out of her deep heart spoke—
    I felt, but heard not.
                 Shelley.

24. Even so with smoothing gentleness began
    The mitred Preacher, winning audience close:
Till, rising up, the rapid argument
    Soared to the Empyrean, linking earth
With heaven by golden chains of eloquence;
    Till the mind, all its faculties and powers,
Lay floating, self-surrendered in the deep
    Of admiration.

Milman.

25. Ah! wherefore all this wormy circumstance?
        Why linger at the yawning tomb so long?
    O for the gentleness of old Romance,
        The simple plaining of a minstrel's song!
    Fair reader, at the old tale take a glance,
        For hear, in truth, it doth not well belong
    To speak:—O turn thee to the very tale,
    And taste the music of that vision pale.
    With duller steel than the Perséan sword
        They cut away no formless monster's head,
    But one whose gentleness did well accord
        With death as life.   The ancient harps have said,
    Love never dies, but lives, immortal lord:
        If Love impersonate was ever dead,
    Pale Isabella kissed it, and low moaned.
    'Twas love; cold,—dead indeed, but not dethroned.

Keats.

26. How sweet the answer Echo makes
        To Music at night,
    When, roused by lute or horn, she wakes;
    And far away, o'er lawns and lakes,
        Goes answering light.

Yet Love hath echoes truer far,
  And far more sweet,
Than e'er, beneath the moonlight's star,
Of horn, or lute, or soft guitar,
  The songs repeat.
'Tis when the sigh in youth sincere,
  And only then,—
The sigh that's breathed for one to hear,
Is by that one, that only dear,
  Breathed back again!

Moore.

27. The cheerful Sabbath bells, wherever heard,
Strike pleasant on the sense, most like the voice
Of one, who from the far-off hills proclaims
Tidings of good to Zion: chiefly when
Their piercing tones fall *sudden* on the ear
Of the contemplant, solitary man,
Whom thoughts abtruse or high have chanced to
  lure
Forth from the walks of men, revolving oft,
And oft again, hard matter, which eludes
And baffles his pursuit—thought-sick and tired
Of controversy, where no end appears,
No clue to his research, the lonely man
Half wishes for society again.
Him, thus engaged, the Sabbath bells salute
Sudden! his heart awakes, his ears drink in
The cheering music; his relenting soul
Yearns after all the joys of social life,
And softens with the love of human kind.

Lamb.

28. Loud was the lightsome tumult of the shore,
    Oft music changed, but never ceased her tone,
    And timely echoed back the measured oar,
    And rippling waters made a pleasant moan:
    The queen of tides on high consenting shone,
    And when a transient breeze swept o'er the wave,
    'Twas, as if darting from her heavenly throne,
    A brighter glance her form reflected gave,
    Till sparkling billows seemed to 'light the banks
        they lave.
                                Byron.

29. There was a sound of revelry by night,
    And Belgium's capital had gathered then
    Her beauty and her chivalry; and bright
    The lamps shone o'er fair women and brave men;
    A thousand hearts beat happily; and when
    Music arose with its voluptuous swell,
    Soft eyes looked love to eyes which spake again,
    And all went merry as a marriage-bell;
    But hush! hark! a deep sound strikes like a rising
        knell.
    Did ye not hear it?—No; 'twas but the wind,
    Or the car rattling o'er the stony street;
    On with the dance! let joy be unconfined,
    No sleep till morn when youth and pleasure meet,
    To chase the glowing hours with flying feet—
    But, hark! that heavy sound breaks in once more,
    As if the clouds its echo would repeat;
    And nearer, clearer, deadlier than before!
    Arm! arm! it is—it is—the cannon's opening roar!
                                Byron.

30. Clear, placid Leman! thy contrasted lake,
With the wild world I dwelt in, is a thing
Which warns me, with its stillness, to forsake
Earth's troubled waters for a purer spring.
This quiet sail is as a noiseless wing
To waft me from distraction; once I loved
Torn ocean's roar, but thy soft murmuring
Sounds sweet as if a sister's voice reproved,
That I with stern delights should e'er have been so
    moved.
                       Byron.

31. It is the hush of night, and all between
Thy margin and the mountains, dusk, yet clear,
Mellowed and mingling, yet distinctly seen,
Save darkened Jura, whose capt heights appear
Precipitously steep; and, drawing near,
There breathes a living fragrance from the shore,
Of flowers yet fresh with childhood; on the ear
Drops the light drip of the suspended oar,
Or chirps the grasshopper one good-night carol
    more:
He is an evening reveller, who makes
His life an infancy, and sings his fill;
At intervals, some bird from out the brakes
Starts into voice a moment, then is still.
There seems a floating whisper on the hill;
But that is fancy, for the starlight dews
All silently their tears of love instil,
Weeping themselves away, till they infuse
Deep into nature's breast the spirit of her hues.
                       Byron.

32. The sky is changed!—and such a change! Oh
      night,
    And storm, and darkness, ye are wondrous strong,
    Yet lovely in your strength, as is the light
    Of a dark eye in woman! Far along,
    From peak to peak, the rattling crags among
    Leaps the live thunder! Not from one lone cloud,
    But every mountain now hath found a tongue,
    And Jura answers, through her misty shroud,
    Back to the joyous Alps, who call to her aloud!
    And this is in the night:—most glorious night!
    Thou wert not sent for slumber! let me be
    A sharer in thy fierce and far delight,—
    A portion of the tempest and of thee!
                                            Byron.

33. A populous solitude of bees and birds,
    And fairy-formed and many-coloured things,
    Who worship him with notes more sweet than words,
    And innocently open their glad wings,
    Fearless and full of life: the gush of springs,
    And fall of lofty fountains and the bend
    Of stirring branches, and the bud which brings
    The swiftest thought of beauty, here extend,
    Mingling, and made by love, unto one mighty end.
                                            Byron.

34.   Alice! one word!
    Let me hear thy voice assuring me of life.
    Ah me! that soft cheek brings me by its touch
    From the black, dizzy, roaring brink of death,
    At once into the heart of happiness!
                                            Wilson.

35. Sweet Mary Gray! thou hast a silver voice,
And wildly to thy native melodies
Can tune its flute-like breath—sing us a song,
And let it be, even mid our merriment,
Most sad, most slow, that when its music dies,
We may address ourselves to revelry,
More passionate from the calm/as men leap up
To this world's business from some heavenly dream.
Wilson.

36. Why hang the sweet bells mute in Magdalene-
Tower,
Still wont to usher in delightful May,
The dewy silence of the morning hour
Cheering with many a changeful roundelay?
And those pure youthful voices, where are they,
That hymning far up in the listening sky,
Seemed issuing softly through the gates of day,
As if a troop of sainted souls on high
Were hovering o'er the earth with angel melody?
Wilson.

37. From the silent heart of a hollow yew,
The owl sailed forth with a loud halloo;
And his large yellow eyes looked bright
With wonder, in the wan moonlight,
As hovering white, and still as snow,
He caught a glance of the things below,
All burning on the bridge like fire
In the sea-green glow of their wild attire.
"Halloo! Halloo! tu-whit! tu-whoo!"
Wilson.

38. Piny wood through which the night wind roars.
Barry Cornwall.

39. Come, Mary Macintyre—give us a song,
Then to our work again.   Thou hast a voice
So sweet that even the linnet on the broom
Might take a lesson from thee.
Wilson.

40. O thou, vast Ocean!   Ever-sounding sea!
Thou symbol of a drear immensity!
Thou thing that windest round the solid world
Like a huge animal, which, downward hurled
From the black clouds, lies weltering and alone,
Lashing and writhing till its strength be gone,
Thy voice is like the thunder, and thy sleep
Is as a giant's slumber, loud and deep.
Barry Cornwall.

41. A sound is in the silent night abroad,
A sound of broken waters.
Milman.

42. Blow music o'er the festal land, from harp
And merry rebeck, till the floating air
Seem harmony; still all fierce sounds of war;
No breath within the clarion's brazen throat;
Soft slumber in the war-steed's drooping mane.
Milman.

43.   Dimly mingling sounds,
Rushing of torrents, roar of prisoned winds.
Milman.

44. That hour, one horn with long and solemn blast
   Went wailing up the heavens; less shrill, less
      drear,
   Blew through the fatal Roncesvalles pass,
   In after times, Roland's deep bugle, heard
   Dolorous, so poets feign, on Paris wall.
   The air seemed shivering where the knell passed on,
   As with a cold wind shuddered the thick trees.
                                    Milman.

45.   The thin whispering leaves,
   The welling water's flow, the lingering, long,
   Love-dwelling descant of the joyous birds
   Came mingling with the languor of his sense,
   Most soothing each in turn, most slumbering soft.
                                    Milman.

46.   Trumpets blown
   Of triumph calm, and hymns of festival
   Upon the gold clouds metropolitan,
   Voices of soft proclaim, and silver stir
   Of strings in hollow shells.
                                    Keats.

47.   Hark!
   'Tis the early April lark.
                                    Keats.

48.   Thou shalt hear
   Distant harvest-carols clear.
                                    Keats.

49. Never did music sink into my soul
So "silver-sweet," as when thy first weak wail
On my rapt ear in doubtful murmurs stole,
Thou child of love and promise! What a tale
Of hopes and fears, of gladness and of gloom,
Hung on that slender filament of sound!
A. A. Wilds.

50. Oh! let me hear that solemn strain again;
It came upon me like the ocean's voice,
Filling me with lofty awe!
Lawrence Holmes.

What Part of the Day do you love?

THE laverock loves the dewy light,
  The bee the balmy foxglove fair;
  The shepherd loves the glowing morn,
  When song and sunshine fill the air:
  But I love best the summer moon,
  With all her stars, pure streaming still;
  For then, in light and love I meet
  The sweet lass of Gleneslan-mill.
                              Cunningham.

2. Awake, my love! ere morning's ray
  Throws off night's weed of pilgrim gray;
  Ere yet the hare, cowered close from view,
  Licks from her fleece the clover dew:
  Or wild swan shakes her snowy wings,
  By hunters roused from secret springs:
  Or birds upon the boughs awake,
  Till green Arbigland's woodlands shake.
                              Cunningham.

3. Till twilight ushers in the summer night:
   And toil reposed, and stars were rising o'er
   The inn's long gallery and its open door.

Hanmer.

4. Now rose the sun, and shy and shamefaced night
   Fled downward from the intolerable light;
   'Neath the broad earth to other stars she goes
   On twilight wings, and seeks her loved repose.

Hanmer.

5. Thou comest to me by morn, my love, and thou art
           brighter far,
   Than the new light.

Hanmer.

6. The morning broke. Light stole upon the clouds
   With a strange beauty. Earth received again
   Its garment of a thousand dyes; and leaves,
   And delicate blossoms, and the painted flowers,
   And every thing that bendeth to the dew,
   And stirreth with the daylight, lifted up
   Its beauty to the breath of that sweet morn.

Willis.

7. Day lit the woody mountains; in the dell
   Were heard the shepherd's song and wether's bell;
   The kid in circles gambolled on the lea,
   And dew, like beauty's tears, empearled each tree;
   The lark, as winged with rapture, sprang on high,
   And sang amidst the roses of the sky:
   Yes, all without was brightness, and a voice
   From wide creation seemed to cry "Rejoice!"

Michell.

8. There is a home-felt stillness in the hour
When heaven's bright azure takes a deeper shade,
And fragrance sleeps in every closing flower;
Then, ere the amber glow is all decayed,
The volume or the work aside is laid,
And the pleased mother views, with glistening eye,
The little games by happy childhood played,
Her fair-haired girls all breathless running by,
With cries of mimic fear and laugh of ecstasy.
When the far clock hath tolled the hour of rest,
They, side by side, before their mother kneel,
And pray their gentle slumbers may be blest,
And their pure spirits dewlike influence feel
Of grace and goodness.—Oh! what raptures steal
Upon a parent's soul at childhood's prayer!
That innocence might all her sorrows heal:
The lifted hands, the features' placid air,
The hymn so sweetly lisped, have all enchantment
    there.
                                        Maldon.

9. Upon that night, so beautiful and mild,
When heaven was all one cloud of stars and dew.
                                        Anon.

10. Hush 'tis a holy hour—the quiet room
    Seems like a temple, while yon soft lamp sheds
A faint and starry radiance through the gloom,
    And the sweet stillness, down on bright young,
    heads,
With all their clustering locks, untouched by care,
And bowed, as flowers are bowed with night in prayer.
                                        Hemans.

11. How aromatic evening grows? The flowers
    And spicy shrubs exhale like onycha;
    Spikenard and henna emulate in sweets.
    Blest hour! which He, who fashioned it so fair,
    So softly glowing, so contemplative,
    Hath set, and sanctified to look on man.
                               Hillhouse.

12. When cats run home and light is come,
      And dew is cold upon the ground,
    And the far-off stream is dumb,
      And the whirring sail goes round,
      And the whirring sail goes round;
    Alone and warming his five wits,
    The white owl in the belfry sits.
                               Tennyson.

13. When merry milkmaids click the latch,
      And rarely smells the new-mown hay,
    And the cock hath sung beneath the thatch
      Twice or thrice his roundelay,
      Twice or thrice his roundelay:
    Alone and warming his five wits,
    The white owl in the belfry sits.
                               Tennyson.

14. I' the glooming light
    Of middle night.
                               Tennyson.

15. Now is done thy long day's work;
    Fold thy palms across thy breast,
    Fold thine arms, turn to thy rest.
                               Tennyson.

16. Though Night hath climbed her peak of highest noon,
  And bitter blasts the screaming autumn whirl,
  All night through archways of the bridgéd pearl,
  And portals of pure silver walks the moon.
  Tennyson.

17. Oh! timely happy, timely wise,
  Hearts that with rising morn arise!
  Eyes that the beam celestial view,
  Which evermore makes all things new!
  New every morning is the love
  Our wakening and uprising prove;
  Through sleep and darkness safely brought,
  Restored to life, and power, and thought.
  Keble.

18. When the soft dews of kindly sleep
  My wearied eyelids gently steep,
  Be my last thought, how sweet to rest
  For ever on my Saviour's breast.
  Abide with me from morn till eve,
  For without Thee I cannot live:
  Abide with me when night is nigh,
  For without Thee I dare not die.
  Keble.

19. 'Tis morning; and the sun, with ruddy orb
  Ascending, fires the horizon; while the clouds,
  That crowd away before the driving wind,
  More ardent as the disk emerges more,
  Resemble most some city in a blaze,
  Seen through the leafless wood.
  Cowper.

20. The mid-day sun, with fiercest glare,
　　Broods o'er the hazy, twinkling air.
　　　　　　　　　　　　　　　　Keble.

21. "Stop, stop, John Gilpin!—Here's the house"—
　　　They all at once did cry;
　　"The dinner waits, and we are tired!"
　　　Said Gilpin—"So am I!"
　　　　　　　　　　　　　　　　Cowper.

22. And oft he traced the uplands to survey,
　　When o'er the sky advanced the kindling dawn,
　　The crimson cloud, blue main, and mountain gray,
　　And lake, dim-gleaming on the smoky lawn:
　　Far to the west the long, long vale withdrawn,
　　Where twilight loves to linger for a while;
　　And now he faintly kens the bounding fawn,
　　And villager abroad at early toil.
　　But lo! the sun appears! and heaven, earth, ocean,
　　　smile.
　　　　　　　　　　　　　　　　Beattie.

23. The night was Winter in his roughest mood;
　　The morning sharp and clear.　But now at noon
　　Upon the southern side of the slant hills,
　　And where the woods fence off the northern blast
　　The season smiles, resigning all its rage,
　　And has the warmth of May.　The vault is blue
　　Without a cloud, and white without a speck
　　The dazzling splendor of the scene below.
　　Again the harmony comes o'er the vale;
　　And through the trees I view the embattled tower,
　　Whence all the music.
　　　　　　　　　　　　　　　　Cowper.

24. Come, Evening, once again, season of peace;
Return, sweet Evening, and continue long!
Methinks I see thee in the streaky west,
With matron step slow moving, while the Night
Treads on thy sweeping train; one hand employed
In letting fall the curtain of repose
On bird and beast, the other charged for man
With sweet oblivion of the cares of day.
Cowper.

25. Just when our drawing-rooms begin to blaze
With lights, by clear reflection multiplied
From many a mirror, in which he of Gath,
Goliath, might have seen his giant bulk
Whole without stooping, towering crest and all,
My pleasures, too, begin. But me perhaps
The glowing hearth may satisfy awhile
With faint illumination, that uplifts
The shadows to the ceiling, there by fits
Dancing uncouthly to the quivering flame.
Not undelightful is an hour to me
So spent in parlour twilight: such a gloom
Suits well the thoughtful or unthinking mind,
The mind contemplative, with some new theme
Pregnant or indisposed alike to all.
Cowper.

26. The Sun was sunk, and after him the star
Of Hesperus, whose office is to bring
Twilight upon the Earth, short arbiter
'Twixt day and night, and now from end to end
Night's hemisphere had veiled the horizon round.
Milton.

27. To hear the lark begin his flight,
And singing startle the dull Night,
From his watch-tower in the skies,
Till the dappled Dawn doth rise;
Then to come, in spite of sorrow,
And at my window bid good-morrow,
Through the sweet-brier, or the vine,
Or the twisted eglantine:
While the cock, with lively din,
Scatters the rear of Darkness thin,
And to the stack or the barn-door
Stoutly struts his dames before;
Oft listening how the hounds and horn
Cheerly rouse the slumbering Morn,
From the side of some hoar hill,
Through the high wood echoing shrill:
Some time walking, not unseen,
By hedge-row elms, on hillocks green,
Right against the eastern-gate
Where the great Sun begins his state,
Robed in flames, and amber light,
The clouds in thousand liveries dight:
While the plowman, near at hand,
Whistles o'er the furrowed land,
And the milkmaid singeth blithe,
And the mower whets his sithe,
And every shepherd tells his tale,
Under the hawthorn in the dale.

Milton.

28. At midnight, when mankind is wrapt in peace,
   And worldly fancy feeds on golden dreams.

Young.

29. Now stir the fire, and close the shutters fast,
    Let fall the curtains, wheel the sofa round,
    And while the bubbling and loud hissing urn
    Throws up a steamy column, and the cups
    That cheer but not inebriate, wait on each,
    So let us welcome peaceful evening in.
    Cowper.

30. Thus, Night, oft see me in thy pale career,
    Till civil-suited Morn appear,
    Not tricked and frounced as she was wont
    With the Attic boy to hunt,
    But kercheft in a comely cloud,
    While rocking winds are piping loud,
    Or ushered with a shower still
    When the gust hath blown his fill,
    Ending on the rustling leaves,
    With minute drops from off the eaves.
    Milton.

31. Now Morn, her rosy steps in the eastern clime
    Advancing, sowed the earth with orient pearl.
    Milton.

32. Now Night in silent state begins to rise,
    And twinkling orbs bestrow the uncloudy skies;
    Her borrowed lustre growing Cynthia lends,
    And on the main a glittering path extends;
    Millions of worlds hang in the spacious air,
    Which round their suns their annual circles steer;
    Sweet contemplation elevates my sense,
    While I survey the works of Providence.
    Gray.

33. When night first bids the twinkling stars appear,
Or with her cloudy vest enwraps the air.

Gay.

34. Ere yet the morn dispels the fleeting mists,
The signal given by the loud trumpet's voice,
Now high in air the imperial standard waves
Emblazoned rich with gold, and glittering gems,
And like a sheet of fire, through the dun gloom
Streaming meteorous.

Somervile.

35. Sol through white curtains shot a timorous ray,
And oped those eyes that must eclipse the day:
Now lap-dogs give themselves the rousing shake,
And sleepless lovers, just at twelve, awake.

Pope.

36. Falsely luxurious, will not man awake;
And, springing from the bed of sloth, enjoy
The cool, the fragrant, and the silent hour,
To meditation due and sacred song?
For is there aught in sleep can charm the wise?
To lie in dead oblivion, losing half
The fleeting moments of too short a life;
Total extinction of the enlightened soul!
Or else to feverish vanity alive,
Wildered, and tossing through distempered dreams?
Who would in such a gloomy state remain
Longer than nature craves; when every Muse
And every blooming pleasure wait without,
To bless the wildly-devious morning walk?

Thomson.

37. Soon as the morning trembles o'er the sky,
And, unperceived, unfolds the spreading day.
Thomson.

38. The lengthened night elapsed, the morning shines
Serene, in all her dewy beauty bright,
Unfolding fair the last autumnal day.
And now the mounting Sun dispels the fog,
The rigid hoar-frost melts before his beam;
And hung on every spray, on every blade
Of grass, the myriad dew-drops twinkle round.
Thomson.

39. And now when busy crowds retire
To take their evening rest,
The hermit trimmed his little fire,
And cheered his pensive guest.
Goldsmith.

40. Sweet was the sound, when oft at evening's close,
Up yonder hill the village murmur rose;
There, as I passed with careless steps and slow,
The mingling notes came softened from below;
The swain responsive as the milk-maid sung,
The sober herd that lowed to meet their young;
The noisy geese that gabbled o'er the pool,
The playful children just let loose from school:
The watch-dog's voice that bayed the whispering
wind,
And the loud laugh that spoke the vacant mind;
These all in sweet confusion sought the shade,
And filled each pause the nightingale had made.
Goldsmith.

41. When morning's twilight-tinctured beam,
   Strikes their low thatch with slanting gleam,
   They rove abroad in ether blue,
   To dip the scythe in fragrant dew;
   The sheaf to bind, the beech to fell,
   That nodding shades a craggy dell.
                  Warton.

42. So oft I have, the evening still,
   At the fountain of a rill,
   Sate upon a flowery bed,
   With my hand beneath my head;
   While strayed my eyes o'er Towy's flood,
   Over mead and over wood,
   From house to house, from hill to hill,
   Till Contemplation had her fill.
                  Dyer.

43. When azure noontide cheers the dædal globe,
   And the blest regent of the golden day
   Rejoices in his bright meridian tower,
   How oft my wishes ask the night's return,
   That best befriends the melancholy mind!
                  Warton.

44. O come then, Melancholy, queen of thought!
   O come, with saintly look and steadfast step,
   From forth thy cave embowered with mournful yew,
   Where ever to the curfew's solemn sound
   Listening thou sitt'st, and with thy cypress bind
   Thy votary's hair, and seal him for thy son.
                  Warton.

"With her, who shares his pleasures and his heart, sweet converse."
Lady's Oracle, p. 157.

45. The morning finds the self-sequestered man
Fresh for his task, intend what task he may.
Whether inclement seasons recommend
His warm but simple home, where he enjoys
With her, who shares his pleasures and his heart,
Sweet converse, sipping calm the fragrant lymph
Which neatly she prepares; then to his book
Well chosen, and not sullenly perused
In selfish silence, but imparted oft,
As aught occurs, that she may smile to hear,
Or turn to nourishment, digested well.

Cowper.

46. Blest be the wild, sequestered shade,
    And blest the day and hour,
Where Peggy's charms I first surveyed,
    When first I felt their power.

Burns.

47. A rose-bud by my early walk,
    Adown a corn-enclosed bawk,
Sae gently bent its thorny stalk,
    All on a dewy morning.
Ere twice the shades o' dawn are fled,
In a' its crimson glory spread,
And drooping rich the dewy head,
    It scents the early morning.

Burns.

48. Sleep'st thou, or wakest thou, fairest creature;
    Rosy morn now lifts his eye,
Numbering ilka bud which Nature
    Waters wi' the tears of joy.

Burns.

49. Hark, the mavis' evening sang
    Sounding Clouden's woods amang;
    Then a faulding let us gang,
      My bonnie dearie.

                                    Burns

50. While larks with little wing
      Fanned the pure air,
    Tasting the breathing spring,
      Forth I did fare:
    Gay the sun's golden eye
    Peeped o'er the mountains high:
    Such thy morn! did I cry,
      Phillis the fair.

                                    Burns.

What Season do you love?

EASON of mists and mellow fruitfulness!
Close bosom-friend of the maturing sun;
Conspiring with him how to load and bless
With fruit the vines that round the thatch-eaves
    run;
To bend with apples the mossed cottage-trees,
And fill all fruit with ripeness to the core;
To swell the gourd, and plump the hazel-shells
With a sweet kernel; to set budding more,
And still more, later flowers for the bees,
Until they think warm days will never cease,
For summer has o'er-brimmed their clammy
    cells.

                         Keats.

2. ' 'Twas the soft season when the sycamore
Bursts in full foliage, and its pensile flower
Doth all the bees with its sweet breath invite.
                         Hanmer.

3.   When the snow falls
          On the old yew tree,
        And the brook brawls
          Like a river free,
        And the cock calls
          Ere the ploughmen see,
    Then come the wandering gipsies to the door,
    And the dogs bark, for they look wild and poor.
                                    Hanmer.

4. But when November came with cloudy blast.
                                    Hanmer.

5. The while comes winter with his frosts behind,
    And stayeth either course, and killeth all the kind.
                                    Hanmer.

6. Young pine, that like a many-plumed cacique,
    Thy tufted head dost in the garden rear,
    'Tis now the first rejoicing April week,
    Now comes the true renewing of the year;
    For all before was winter stern and drear
    Warming his hands, where Time (like Saturn old
    Devouring his own race) some woodland peer
    Heaped on the fire, to save him from the cold;
    And men beside of storms sad stories told,
    The shipwrecks, and the sea-salt on the panes.
    Now all the chestnuts their great buds unfold,
    And that unloving season but remains
    In sight, like some black hill we leave behind,
    South steering with a fair and sunny wind.
                                    Hanmer.

7. It is the winter, sharp and suddenly
   His angel frost hath breathed upon the land.
                                        Hanmer.

8. Lo! from beyond the chill and dusky north,
   The primal month, which leads the rolling year.
                                        Boker.

9. Now to its second term strides on the year,
   And lengthening days foretell mild spring is near.
   One day's warm sunshine clears the frozen earth
   Of ice and snow, until another birth
   Of the rough north whitens the softening land,
   And binds the plains and streams in winter's
       numbing band.
                                        Boker.

10. March the reeling trees is shaking,
    And their withered twigs is breaking
        In his nervous hand;
    While the new loosed streams are dashing,
    Round their rocky barriers flashing;   ⸱
        Or the frost-rent strand
    Crumbles 'neath their furious rushing,
    And above the banks they're gushing
        Deluging the land.
                                        Boker.

11. To April glides the changing year,
        The month which laughs amid her frown;
    Now on her lids there hangs a tear,
        Or weltering showers the meadows drown;
                                11

Then half a smile the earth cheers up,
    And nectarous draughts the sunbeams quaff
From the young blossom's brimming cup;
    Or, with one universal laugh,
Nature's young, giddy scions shout.
    Birds scream from out the dancing trees;
The blue-eyed violets wink about,
    And toss their odours on the breeze;
The gurgling streams suck in the springs,
    And seem to leap along more fleet;
As on the rocky pathway rings
    Sound of their twinkling silver feet;
The grass steals forth with face all wan,
    By the life-giving sun beguiled,
To see if surly March is gone—
    All Nature, like a new-born child,
Leaps on its fruitful mother's lap,
    To win by its innoxious wiles—
If such a gracious thing may hap—
    Its great Creator's golden smiles:
For there's a glory in the hour
    Beyond what e'en the sun can lend,
Beyond the grass and opening flower,
    A something in which heaven must blend.

                            Boker.

12. What Witch could shape this balmy day
    But buxom, blue-eyed, sweet-breathed May!
    Peeping from the roses sheen,
    Peeping from the grasses green,
    Peeping through the ether blue,
    And heard when shouts the blithe cuckoo;

Or when the blue-bird's quivering cry
Drops, like a sunheam, from the sky;
Or when the swallow's scolding note
Seems in the very ear to float,
Then, in a moment, far away,
You scarce can catch its distant lay.
All is life, and all is joy!

Boker.

13. June, when roses deck the ground,
Scatters sweetest smells around;
Flowers which choicest breath exhale,
Bushes, trees, and vines that trail
On trellis or along the ground,
In full-blown majesty abound.
Birds, within the close-leaved groves,
Whisper to their near perched loves;
'Neath the graceful panther steals
Purring at his coy dame's heels;
While the now all-fearless deer
His agile foeman passes near,
Trailing towards the herded does;
Or, with locked horns, and sharp hoof's blows,
Wrestles with some rival bold,
Tangled in his antler's hold.

Boker.

14. At last, mid bleak December's awful ice,
The earth-worn wanderer sadly sits him down.
But earthly joys no longer him entice,
Eternal thoughts his palsied senses drown,
And gathering doubts around him darkly frown.

Boker.

15. The yellow leaves which now appear
    Upon the trees' green heads,
  Like those first warnings, wan and drear,
    Which Time departing spreads
  Among the locks, from day to day,
    To warn us of the tomb,
  Foretell how autumn's slow decay
    Shall rob them of their bloom.

Boker.

16. I see thee springing in the vernal time,
    A sapling weak from out the barren stone,
    To dance with May upon the mountain peak;
    Pale leaves put forth to greet the genial clime,
    And roots shoot down life's sustenance to seek,
    While mere existence was a joy alone.

Boker.

17 A spirit haunts the year's last hours
    Dwelling amid these yellowing bowers:
      To himself he talks;
    For at eventide, listening earnestly,
    At his work you may hear him sob and sigh
      In the walks;
    Earthward he boweth the heavy stalks
  Of the mouldering flowers:
    Heavily hangs the broad sunflower
      Over its grave in the earth so chilly;
    Heavily hangs the hollyhock,
      Heavily hangs the tiger-lily.

Tennyson.

MAY MORNING.

"To dance with May upon the mountain peak."

Lady's Oracle, p. 164.

18.   How full of life,
The life of song, and breezes, and free wings,
Is all the murmuring shade! and thine, O *thine!*
Of all the brightest and the happiest here,
My blessed child! *my* gift of God! that makest
My heart o'erflow with summer!
                                   Hemans.

19. Where sucks the bee now?   Summer is flying,
Leaves on the grass-plot faded are lying;
Violets are gone from the grassy dell,
With the cowslip-cups where the fairies dwell;
The rose from the garden hath passed away.
                                   Hemans.

20. Old Winter's last greeting,
As slowly retreating,
Snow flying, hail beating;
   The warrior grim
His last stand is making,
His last lance is breaking,
His last vengeance taking,
   His glories grow dim.
                                   Boker.

21. Oh day of days! shall hearts set free
No "minstrel rapture" find for Thee?
Thou art the Sun of other days,
They shine by giving back thy rays:
Enthroned in thy sovereign sphere
Thou shedd'st thy light on all the year:
Sundays by Thee more glorious break,
An Easter Day in every week.
                                   Keble.

22. Not till the freezing blast is still,
    Till freely leaps the sparkling rill,
    And gales sweep soft from summer skies,
    As o'er a sleeping infant's eyes
    A mother's kiss; ere calls like these,
    No sunny gleam awakes the trees,
    Nor dare the tender flowerets show
    Their bosoms to the uncertain glow.

                                    Keble.

23. Well may I guss and feel
        Why Autumn should be sad;
    But vernal airs should sorrow heal,
        Spring should be gay and glad.

                                    Keble.

24. It was the winter wild,
        While the heaven-born child
        All meanly wrapt in the rude manger lies,
    Nature in awe to him
    Has doffed her gaudy trim,
        With her great Master so to sympathize:
    It was no season then for her
    To wanton with the Sun, her lusty paramour.

                                    Milton.

25. In simmer when the hay was mawn,
        And corn waved green in ilka field,
    While claver blooms white o'er the lea,
        And roses blaw in ilka bield.

                                    Burns.

26 The clouds that wrap the setting sun
   When autumn's softest gleams are ending,
Where all bright hues together run
   In sweet confusion blending:—
Why, as we watch their floating wreath,
Seem they the breath of life to breathe?
To Fancy's eye their motions prove
They mantle round the sun for love.
Keble.

27. Red o'er the forest peers the setting sun,
   The line of yellow light dies fast away
That crowned the eastern copse; and chill and dun
   Falls on the moor the brief November day.
Keble.

28. Who says, the wan autumnal sun
   Beams with too faint a smile
To light up nature's face again,
And, though the year be on the wane,
   With thoughts of spring the heart beguile?
Waft him, thou soft September breeze,
   And gently lay him down
Within some circling woodland wall,
Where bright leaves, reddening ere they fall,
   Wave gayly o'er the waters brown.
And let some graceful arch be there
   With wreathed mullions proud,
With burnished ivy for its screen,
And moss, that glows as fresh and green
   As though beneath an April cloud.
Keble.

29. Soon o'er their heads blithe April airs shall sing,
    A thousand wild-flowers round them shall unfold,
The green buds glisten in the dews of spring,
    And all be vernal rapture as of old.
                     Keble.

30. Dear is the morning gale of spring,
    And dear the autumnal eve;
But few delights can summer bring
    A poet's crown to weave.
Her bowers are mute, her fountains dry,
    And ever Fancy's wing
Speeds from beneath her cloudless sky,
    To autumn or to spring.
                     Keble.

31. Why blow'st thou not, thou wintry wind,
    Now every leaf is brown and sere,
And idly droops, to thee resigned,
    The fading chaplet of the year?
Yet wears the pure aerial sky
Her summer veil, half drawn on high,
Of silvery haze, and dark and still
The shadows sleep on every slanting hill.
                     Keble.

32. Mindful of disaster past,
    And shrinking at the northern blast,
The sleety storm returning still,
The morning hoar, and evening chill;
Reluctant comes the timid spring.
                     Warton.

33. O Winter, ruler of the inverted year,
    Thy scattered hair with sleet like ashes filled,
    Thy breath congealed upon thy lips, thy cheeks
    Fringed with a beard made white with other snows
    Than those of age, thy forehead wrapped in clouds,
    A leafless branch thy sceptre, and thy throne
    A sliding car, indebted to no wheels,
    But urged by storms along its slippery way,
    I love thee, all unlovely as thou seem'st,
    And dreaded as thou art!
                       Cowper.

34. Pale humid winter loves the generous board,
    The meal more copious, and the warmer fare;
    And longs with old wood and old wine to cheer
    His quaking heart.
                       Armstrong.   .

35. Through autumn's languishing domain
    Descending, Nature by degrees invites
    To glowing luxury.
                       Armstrong.

36. When the fresh spring in all her state is crowned,
    And high luxuriant grass o'erspreads the ground.
                       Gay.

37. Now golden autumn from her open lap
    Her fragrant bounties showers; the fields are shorn;
    Inwardly smiling, the proud farmer views
    The rising pyramids that grace his yard,
    And counts his large increase; his barns are stored
    And groaning staddles bend beneath their load.
                       Somervile.

38. Ere yet the sun through the bright Ram has urged
    His steepy course, or mother Earth unbound
    Her frozen bosom to the western gale;
    When feathered troops, their social leagues dis-
            solved,
    Select their mates, and on the leafless elm
    The noisy rook builds high her wicker nest.
    Somervile.

39. In that soft season, when descending showers
    Call forth the greens, and wake the rising flowers;
    When opening buds salute the welcome day,
    And earth relenting feels the genial ray;
    As balmy sleep had charmed my cares to rest,
    And love itself was banished from my breast,
    (What time the morn mysterious visions brings,
    While purer slumbers spread their golden wings,)
    A train of phantoms in wild order rose,
    And joined, this intellectual scene compose.
    Pope.

40. Home, from his morning task, the swain retreats,
    His flock before him stepping to the fold:
    While the full-uddered mother lows around
    The cheerful cottage, then expecting food,
    The food of innocence and health!   The daw,
    The rook, and magpie, to the gray-grown oaks
    That the calm village in their verdant arms,
    Sheltering, embrace, direct their lazy flight;
    Where on the mingling boughs they sit embowered,
    All the hot noon, till cooler hours arise.
    Thomson.

41. From brightening fields of ether fair disclosed,
Child of the sun, refulgent summer comes,
In pride of youth, and felt through nature's depth:
He comes attended by the sultry hours,
And ever-fanning breezes, on his way;
While from his ardent look the turning spring
Averts her blushful face; and earth and skies,
All smiling, to his hot dominion leaves.
Thomson.

42. Crowned with the sickle and the wheaten sheaf,
While'autumn, nodding o'er the yellow plain,
Comes jovial on.
Thomson.

43. Hence from the busy joy-resounding fields,
In cheerful error, let us tread the maze
Of autumn unconfined; and taste, revived,
The breath of orchard big with bending fruit.
Obedient to the breeze and beating ray,
From the deep-loaded bough a mellow shower
Incessant melts away.
Thomson.

44. Now all amid the rigours of the year,
In the wild depth of winter, while without
The ceaseless winds blow ice, be my retreat,
Between the groaning forest and the shore,
Beat by the boundless multitude of waves,
A rural, sheltered, solitary scene;
Where ruddy fire and beaming tapers join,
To cheer the gloom.
Thomson.

45. See winter comes, to rule the varied year,
    Sullen and sad, with all his rising train,
    Vapours, and clouds, and storms. Be these my
        theme!
    These! that exalt the soul to solemn thought,
    And heavenly musing. Welcome, kindred glooms!
    Congenial horrors, hail! with frequent foot,
    Pleased have I, in my cheerful morn of life,
    When nursed by careless solitude I lived,
    And sung of Nature with unceasing joy,
    Pleased have I wandered through your rough
        domain;
    Trod the pure virgin-snows, myself as pure;
    Heard the winds roar, and the big torrent burst;
    Or seen the deep fermenting tempest brewed
    In the grim evening sky. Thus passed the time,
    Till through the lucid chambers of the south
    Looked out the joyous spring, looked out and smiled.
                            Thomson.

46. Now when the cheerless empire of the sky
    To Capricorn the Centaur Archer yields,
    And fierce Aquarius stains the inverted year;
    Hung o'er the farthest verge of heaven, the sun
    Scarce spreads through ether the dejected day.
    Faint are his gleams, and ineffectual shoot
    His struggling rays, in horizontal lines,
    Through the thick air; as, clothed in cloudy storm,
    Weak, wan, and broad, he skirts the southern sky;
    And, soon descending, to the long dark night,
    Wide-shading all, the prostrate world resigns.
                            Thomson.

47. Let others love soft summer's evening smiles,
As, listening to the distant water-fall,
They mark the blushes of the streaky west;
I choose the pale December's foggy glooms.
Then, when the sullen shades of evening close,
Where through the room a blindly· glimmering
　gleam
The dying embers scatter, far remote
From Mirth's mad shouts, that through the illumined
　roof
Resound with festive echo, let me sit,
Blest with the lowly cricket's drowsy dirge.
Then let my thought contemplative explore
This fleeting state of things, the vain delights,
The fruitless toils, that still our search elude,
As through the wilderness of life we rove.
　　　　　　　　　　　　　　　Warton.

48. O May, thy morn was ne'er sae sweet
As the mirk night o' December.
　　　　　　　　　　　　　　　Burns.

49. The smiling spring comes in rejoicing,
　And surly winter grimly flies:
Now crystal clear are the falling waters,
　And bonnie blue are the sunny skies;
Fresh o'er the mountains breaks forth the morn-
　ing,
　The evening gilds the ocean's swell,
All creatures joy in the sun's returning,
　And I rejoice in my bonnie Bell.
　　　　　　　　　　　　　　　Burns.

50. Lessons sweet of spring returning,
    Welcome to the thoughtful heart!
May I call ye sense or learning,
    Instinct pure, or heaven-taught art?
Be your title what it may,
Sweet and lengthening April day,
While with you the soul is free,
Ranging wild o'er hill and lea.

                           Keble.

What is your favourite Flower?

—

HERE'S the lily of the vale,
That perfumed the morning gale,
My fairy Mary Lee!
All so spotless and so pale,
Like thine own purity.
And, might I make it known,
'Tis an emblem of my own
Love—if I dare so name
My esteem for thee.
Surely flowers can bear no blame,
My bonny Mary Lee!

John Clare.

2. Here's the violet, modest blue,
That 'neath hawthorns hides from view,
My gentle Mary Lee,
Would show whose heart is true,
While it thinks of thee.
While they choose each lowly spot,
The sun disdains them not;

I'm as lowly, too, indeed,
   My charming Mary Lee,
So I've brought the flowers to plead,
   And win a smile from thee.

Clare.

3. Here's a wild rose just in bud;
   Spring's beauty in its hood,
     My bonny Mary Lee!
'Tis the first in all the wood
   I could find for thee.
Though a blush is scarcely seen,
Yet it hides its worth within,
Like my love; for I've no power,
   My angel, Mary Lee,
To speak, unless the flower
   Can make excuse for me.

Clare.

4. We are slumbering poppies,
   Lords of Lethe downs,
Some awake, and some asleep,
   Sleeping in our crowns.
What perchance our dreams may know,
Let our serious beauty show.
Central depth of purple,
   Leaves more bright than rose,—
Who shall tell what brightest thought
   Out of darkest grows?
Who, through what funereal pain,
Souls to love and peace attain?

Leigh Hunt.

5. We are blushing roses,
   Bending with our fulness,
   Midst our close-capped sister buds
   Warming the green coolness.
   Whatsoe'er of beauty
   Yearns and yet reposes,
   Blush, and bosom, and sweet breath,
   Took a shape in roses.
   Hold one of us lightly,—
   See from what a slender
   Stalk we bower in heavy blooms,
   And roundness rich and tender:
   Know you not our only
   Rival flower,—the human?
   Loveliest weight on lightest foot,
   Joy-abundant woman?

   Hunt.

6. Ye field flowers! the gardens eclipse you, 'tis true,
   Yet, wildings of nature, I dote upon you,
      For ye waft me to summers of old,
   When the earth teemed around me with fairy delight,
   And when daisies and buttercups gladdened my sight,
      Like treasures of silver and gold.

   Campbell.

7. The rose was rich in bloom on Sharon's plain.

   Hemans.

8.   Laburnum, rich
   In streaming gold.

   Cowper.

12

9. We are lilies fair,
    The flower of virgin light;
Nature held us forth, and said,
    "Lo! my thoughts of white."
Ever since then, angels
    Hold us in their hands;
You may see them where they take
    In pictures their sweet stands.
Like the garden's angels
    Also do we seem;
And not the less for being crowned
    With a golden dream.
Could you see around us
    The enamoured air,
You would see it pale with bliss
    To hold a thing so fair.

Hunt.

10. Copious of flowers the woodbine, pale and wan,
    But well compensating her sickly looks
    With never-cloying odours, early and laté.

Cowper.

11. Hypericum, all bloom, so thick a swarm
   Of flowers, like flies clothing her slender rods,
    That scarce a leaf appears.

Cowper.

12.   Mezereon, too,
    Though leafless, well attired, and thick beset
    With blushing wreaths, investing every spray.

Cowper.

13. The lilac, various in array, now white,
Now sanguine, and her beauteous head now set
With purple spikes pyramidal, as if
Studious of ornament, yet unresolved
Which hue she most approved, she chose them all;
                                        Cowper.

14.   The broom
Yellow and bright, as bullion unalloyed,
Her blossoms.
                                        Cowper.

15.   Luxuriant above all,
The jasmine, throwing wide her elegant sweets,
The deep dark green of whose unvarnished leaf
Makes more conspicuous, and illumines more
The bright profusion of her scattered stars.
                                        Cowper.

16. A beam upon the myrtle fell
     From dewy evening's purest sky,
'Twas like the glance I love so well,
     Dear Eva, from thy moonlight eye.
I looked around the summer grove,
     On every tree its lustre shone;
For all had felt that look of love
     The silly myrtle deemed its own.
Eva! behold thine image there,
     As fair, as false thy glances fall;
But who the worthless smile would share
     That sheds its light alike on all?
                                        Drake.

17. Our rocks are rough, but smiling there
    The acacia waves her yellow hair,
    Lonely and sweet, nor loved the less
    For flowering in a wilderness——
    Then come—thy Arab maid will be
    The loved and lone acacia tree.
                                        Moore.

18. Cowslips wan that hang the pensive head.
                                        Milton.

19. The slender bryony that weaves
    His pale green flowers and glossy leaves
    Aloft in smooth and lithe festoons;
    And crowned compact with yellow cones,
    Mid purple petals dropped with green,
    The woody nightshade climbs between.
                                        Mant.

20. Sweet blooms genista in the myrtle shade.
                                        Darwin.

21. With solemn adoration down they cast
    Their crowns, inwove with amaranth and gold;
    Immortal amaranth, a flower which once
    In Paradise, fast by the tree of life,
    Began to bloom; but soon for man's offence
    To heaven removed, where first it grew, there grows,
    And flowers aloft, shading the fount of life,
    And where the river of bliss through midst of heaven
    Rolls o'er Elysian flowers her amber stream,
    With those that never fade.
                                        Milton.

22.   Nightshade's purple flowers,
Hanging so sleepily their turbaned heads,
Rested upon the hedge.

Twamley.

23.   I wander out and rhyme;
What hour the dewy morning's infancy
Hangs on each blade of grass and every tree,
And sprents the red thighs of the humble bee,
Who 'gins betimes unwearied minstrelsy;
Who breakfasts, dines, and most divinely sups,
With every flower save golden buttercups,—
On whose proud bosoms he will never go,
But passes by with scarcely "how do ye do,"
Since in their showy, shining, gaudy cells
Haply the summer's honey never dwells.

Clare.

24. When once the sun sinks in the west,
And dew-drops pearl the evening's breast;
Almost as pale as moonbeams are,
Or its companionable star,
The evening primrose opes anew
Its delicate blossoms to the dew;
And, hermit-like, shunning the light,
Wastes its fair bloom upon the Night,
Who, blindfold to its fond caresses,
Knows not the beauty he possesses.
Thus it blooms on while Night is by;
When Day looks out with open eye,
'Bashed at the gaze it cannot shun,
It faints, and withers, and is gone.

Clare.

TRAVELLER'S JOY.

25.   Who gave to thee that name,
     So full of homely and most pleasant thought?
       Its charm might win renown
     For many a thing with far less beauty fraught.
       There's something in it tells
     Of wanderings ended brightly;—of the close,
       Mid old familiar scenes,
     Of the tired wayfarer's amount of woes.
       Wert thou the humblest flower
     That we e'er scorn with that rude term, "a weed,"
       Thy *name* would unto me
     For kindly thought and pleasant fancies plead.
       But thou art beautiful,
     And our sole native of thy graceful band,
       Which we so prize, and seek,
     In varied form and hue, through many a land.
       How often have I paused,
     A joyous traveller, in sooth to cull
       A garland of thy flowers,
     When with faint sweets the sun had filled them full.
                       Twamley.

26. The cranberry blossom dwelleth there
   . Amid the mountains cold,
  Seeming like a fairy gift
    Left on the dreary wold.
  Oh! and 'tis very beautiful,
    The flowers are pink and white,
  And the small oval polished leaves
    Are evergreen and bright.

'Tis such a wee, fair, dainty thing,
  You'd think a greenhouse warm
Would be its proper dwelling-place,
  Kept close from wind and storm.
But on the moors it dwelleth free
  Like a fearless mountain child;
With a rosy cheek, a lightsome look,
  And a spirit strong and wild.
The bushes all in water grow,
  In those small pools that lie
In scores among the turfy knolls
  On mountains broad and high.
                                        Twamley.

27. O reader! hast thou ever stood to see
    The holly tree?
    The eye that contemplates it well perceives
    Its glossy leaves;
    Ordered by an Intelligence so wise
    As might confound an atheist's sophistries.
    Below a circling fence its leaves are seen
    Wrinkled and keen!
    No grazing cattle through their prickly round
    Can reach to wound;
    But, as they grow where nothing is to fear,
    Smooth and unarmed the pointless leaves appear.
                                        Southey.

28. Thine full many a pleasing bloom
    Of blossoms lost to all perfume;
    Thine the dandelion flowers,
    Gilt with dew like sun with showers.
                                        Clare.

29. Like to an almond-tree, mounted high
    On top of green Selinis, all alone,
    With blossoms brave bedecked daintily;
    Whose tender locks do tremble every one,
    At every little breath that under heaven is blown.
    Spenser.

30. Bring lilies for a maiden's grave,
        Roses to deck the bride,
    Tulips for all who love through life
        In brave attire to ride:
    Bring each for each, in bower and hall,
    But cull the columbine for all.
    The columbine?   Full many a flower
        Hath hues more clear and bright,
    Although she doth in purple go,
        In crimson, pink, and white.
    Why, when so many fairer shine
    Why choose the homely columbine?
    Know ye the cap which Folly wears
        In ancient masques and plays?
    Does not the columbine recall
        That toy of olden days?
    And is not Folly reigning now
    O'er many a wisdom-written brow?
    'Tis Folly's flower, that homely one;
        That universal guest
    Makes every garden but a type
        Of every human breast;
    For though ye tend both mind and bower,
    There's still a nook for Folly's flower.
    Twamley.

31. On scaly stem, with cottony down,
O'erlaid, its lemon-coloured crown,
Which drooped unclosed, but now erect,
The colts-foot bright develops; decked
(Ere yet the impurpled stalk displays
Its dark green leaves) with countless rays,
Round countless tubes, alike in dye,
Expanded.

Mant.

32. Yonder is a girl who lingers
Where wild honeysuckle grows,
Mingled with the brier rose.

H. Smith.

33. A sweeter spot on earth was never found:
I looked, and looked, and still with new delight;
Such joy my soul, such pleasures filled my sight;
And the fresh eglantine exhaled a breath,
Whose odours were of power to raise from death.

Dryden.

34. The green and graceful fern,
How beautiful it is!
There's not a leaf in all the land
So wonderful, I wis.
Have ye ever watched it budding,
With each stem and leaf wrapped small,
Coiled up within each other
Like a round and hairy ball?
Have ye watched that ball unfolding
Each closely nestling curl,
And its fair and feathery leaflets
Their spreading forms unfurl?

Oh! then most gracefully they wave
  In the forest, like a sea,
And dear as they are beautiful,
  Are these fern leaves to me.
For all of early childhood—
  Those past and blessed years
To which we ever wistfully
  Look back through memory's tears—
The sports and fancies then my own,
  Those fern leaves dear and wild
Bring back to my delighted breast—
  I am once more a child.

                    Twamley.

35. Fair maidens, I'll sing you a song;
  I'll tell you the bonny wild flower,
Whose blossoms so yellow, and branches so long,
O'er moor and o'er rough rocky mountain are flung,
  Far away from trim garden and bower.
It clings to the crag, and it clothes the wild hill;
  It stands sturdily breasting the storm,
When the loud-voiced winds sing so drearily shrill,
And the snow-flakes in eddies fall silent and still,
  And the shepherd can scarce wrap him warm.
'Tis the bonny bright gorse, that gleams cheerily
     forth,
  Like sunlight e'er lingering here,
In the verdure of spring, and when summer on
     earth
Has called all the fairest of blossoms to birth,
  As a crown for the noon of the year.

                    Twamley.

36. The foxgloves and the fern,
    How gracefully they grow,
With grand old oaks above them
    And wavy grass below!
The stately trees stand round
    Like columns fair and high,
And the spreading branches bear
    A glorious canopy
Of leaves, that rustling wave
    In the whispering summer air,
And gayly greet the sunbeams
    That are falling brightly there.
The miser-leaves!—they suffer
    Not a gleam to twinkle through,
And in the foxglove's hairy cup,
    At noonday, drops of dew
Are hanging round like tears
    Of sorrow, that the sun
Gives to other flowers his kisses,
    But to her soft lips not one.
                    Twamley.

37. Oh! come to the river's rim, come with us there,
For the white water-lily is wondrous fair,
With her large broad leaves on the stream afloat,
Each one a capacious fairy-boat.
The swan among flowers! How stately ride
Her snow-white leaves on the glittering tide!
And the dragon-fly gallantly stays to sip
A kiss of dew from her goblet's lip.
                    Twamley.

38. Hawthorn, famed mid vernal scene
  For gracing May's propitious hour
  With prodigality of flower,
  Pink-anthered mid its petals pale,
  And lending fragrance to the gale;
  Hailed from its fair and sweet array
  The namesake of the lovely May.

  Twamley.

39. And thou, so rich in gentle names, appealing
    To hearts that own our nature's common lot;
  Those, styled by sportive fancy's better feeling,
    A Thought, The Heart's Ease, or Forget me not
  Barton.

40.   The erica here,
  That o'er the Caledonian hills sublime
  Spreads its dark mantle, (where the bees delight
  To seek their purest honey,) flourishes;
  Sometimes with bells like amethysts, and then,
  Paler, and shaded like the maiden's cheek
  With gradual blushes—other while, as white
  As rime that hangs upon the frozen spray.
  Of this, old Scotia's hardy mountaineers
  Their rustic couches form; and there enjoy
  Sleep, which, beneath his velvet canopy,
  Luxurious idleness implores in vain.

  Twamley.

41. Ah! 'tis a goodly little thing,
    It groweth for the poor,
  And many a peasant blesses it,
    Beside his cottage door.

He thinketh how those slender stems
   That shimmer in the sun,
Are rich for him in web and woof,
   And shortly shall be spun.
He thinketh how those tender flowers
   Of seed will yield him store;
And sees in thought his next year's crop,
   Blue, shining round his door.
Oh! the goodly flax-flower!
   It groweth on the hill;
And be the breeze awake or sleep,
   It never standeth still!
It seemeth all astir with life,
   As if it loved to thrive,
As if it had a merry heart
   Within its stem alive!
Then fair befall the flax-field;
   And may the kindly showers
Give strength unto its shining stems,
   Give seed unto its flowers.
                              Mary Howitt.

42. Why this flower is now called so,
    List, sweet maids, and you shall know.
    Understand, this firstling was
    Once a brisk and bonny lasse,
    (Kept as close as Danaë was;)
    Who a sprightly springall loved,
    And, to have it fully proved,
    Up she got upon a wall,
    Tempting down to slide withall;
    But the silken twist untied,
    So she fell, and, bruised, she died.

Love, in pity of the deed,
And her loving lucklesse speed,
Changed her to this plant, we call
Now, the Flower of the Wall.

Herrick.

43. Sweet violets, Love's paradise, that spread
   Your gracious odours, which you couched bear
     Within your paly faces,
Upon the gentle wing of some calm-breathing wind
     That plays amidst the plain;
  If, by the favour of propitious stars, you gain
Such grace as in my lady's bosom place to find,
   Be proud to touch those places.

Scott.

44. I'll go and peep at the pimpernel,
   And see if she think the clouds look well;
     For if the sun shine,
     And 'tis like to be fine,
     I shall go to the fair,
     For my sweetheart is there:
So, pimpernel, what bode the clouds and the sky?
If fair weather, no maiden so merry as I.
Now the pimpernel-flower had folded up
Her little gold star in her coral cup,
     And unto the maid
     Thus her warning said:
     Though the sun smile down,
     There's a gathering frown
O'er the checkered blue of the clouded sky;
So tarry at home, for a storm is nigh.

Twamley.

45. The tuberose, with her silver light,
　　That in the garden of Malay
　Is called the mistress of the night;
　So like a bride, scented and bright,
　　She comes out when the sun's away.

Moore.

46. It was the tall, sweet-scented flag,
　　Lay pictured there so true,
　I could have deemed some fairy hand
　　The faithful image drew.
　The falchion-leaves, all long and sharp;
　　The stem, like a tall leaf too,
　Except where, halfway up its side,
　　A cone-shaped flowerspike grew.
　Like a lady's finger, taper, long,
　　From end to end arrayed
　In close scale-armour, that was all
　　Of starry flowers made.
　If you could fancy fairy folk
　　Would mimic work of ours,
　You'd think their dainty fingers here
　　Had wrought mosaic flowers.
　The tiny petals neatly formed,
　　With geometric skill,
　Are each one so exactly shaped,
　　Its proper place to fill.
　And stamens, like fine golden dust,
　　Spangle the flowerets green;
　Aught more compact or beautiful
　　Mine eyes have never seen!

Twamley.

47. No flower amid the garden fairer grows
   Than the sweet lily of the lowly vale,
   The queen of flowers.

Keats.

48.   EMILIA.—Of all flowers,
Methinks a rose is best.
     SERVANT.—Why, gentle madam?
     EMILIA.—It is the very emblem of a maid:
For when the west wind courts her gently,
How modestly she blows, and paints the sun
With her chaste blushes! When the north comes
     near her,
Rude and impatient, then, like chastity,
She locks her beauties in her bud again,
And leaves him to base friars.

Beaumont.

49. The blue-eyed forget-me-not, beautiful flower,
   Half-wooed and half-stolen, I brought from her
     bower,
   By the bright river's brink, where she nestled so
     low,
   That the water o'er stem and o'er leaflet might flow;
   As if, like Narcissus, she foolishly tried
   To gaze on her own gentle face in the tide.
   Half inclined, half reluctant, the flower bade adieu
   To the friends left behind in the dell where she grew;
   And a few shining drops, from the river-spray flung,
   Like tears of regret on her azure eyes hung;
   But I kissed them away, as a lover had done,
   In joy that my fair river-beauty I'd won.

Twamley.

50. Around the door the honeysuckle climbed,
   . And multiflora spread her countless roses,
  And never minstrel sang nor poet rhymed
    Romantic scene where happiness reposes,
  Sweeter to sense than that enchanting dell
  Where home-sick memory fondly loves to dwell.
Anon.

Which is your favourite Dramatic Character?

NGELO,
There is a kind of character in thy life,
That, to the observer, doth thy history
Fully unfold: Thyself and thy belongings
Are not thine own so proper, as to waste
Thyself upon thy virtues, them on thee.
Heaven doth with us, as we with torches do;
Not light them for themselves: for if our
      virtues
Did not go forth with us, 'twere all alike
As if we had them not.   Spirits are not finely
      touched,
But to fine issues: nor nature never lends
The smallest scruple of her excellence,
But, like a thrifty goddess, she determines
Herself the glory of a creditor,
Both thanks and use.

Shakspeare.

194

2. *Shylock*, the world thinks, and I think so too,
That thou but leadest this fashion of thy malice
To the last hour of act; and then, 'tis thought,
Thou'lt show thy mercy, and remorse more strange
Than is thy strange apparent cruelty:
And, where thou now exact'st the penalty,
(Which is a pound of this poor merchant's flesh,)
Thou wilt not only lose the forfeiture,
But, touched with human gentleness and love,
Forgive a moiety of the principal;
Glancing an eye of pity on his losses,
That have of late so huddled on his back;
Enough to press a royal merchant down,
And pluck commiseration of his state
From brassy bosoms and rough hearts of flint,
From stubborn Turks and Tartars never trained
To offices of tender courtesy.
We all expect a gentle answer, Jew.
Shakspeare.

3 *Rosalind* lacks then the love
Which teacheth thee that thou and I am one:
Shall we be sundered? shall we part, sweet girl?
No; let my father seek another heir.
Therefore devise with me, how we may fly,
Whither to go, and what to bear with us:
And do not seek to take your change upon you,
To bear your griefs yourself, and leave me out;
For, by this heaven, now at our sorrow's pale,
Say what thou canst, I'll go along with thee.
Shakspeare

4. Why, *Petruchio* is coming, in a new hat, and an old jerkin; a pair of old breeches, thrice turned; a pair of boots that had been candle-cases, one buckled, another laced; an old rusty sword ta'en out of the town armory, with a broken hilt, and chapeless, with two broken points: His horse hiped with an old mothy saddle, the stirrups of no kindred: besides, possessed with the glanders, and like to mose in the chine; troubled with the lampass, infected with the fashions, full of wind-galls, sped with spavins, raied with the yellows, past cure of the fives, stark spoiled with the staggers, be-gnawn with the bots; swayed in the back, and shoulder-shotten; near legged before, and with a half-checked bit, and a headstall of sheep's leather; which being restrained to keep him from stumbling, hath been often burst, and now repaired with knots; one girt six times pierced, and a woman's crupper of velure, which hath two letters for her name, fairly set down in studs, and here and there pieced with packthread.

Shakspeare.

5. In faith; for you are called plain *Kate*,
    And bonny Kate, and sometimes Kate the curst;
But Kate, the prettiest Kate in Christendom,
Kate of Kate-hall, my super-dainty Kate,
For dainties are all cates: and therefore, Kate,
Take this of me, Kate of my consolation;—
Hearing thy mildness praised in every town,
Thy virtues spoke of and thy beauties sounded,
(Yet not so deeply as to thee belongs,)
Myself am moved to woo thee for my wife.

Shakspeare.

6.   O sweet *Portia,*
Here are a few of the unpleasantest words
That ever blotted paper! Gentle lady,
When I did first impart my love to you,
I freely told you, all the wealth I had
Ran in my veins, I was a gentleman;
And then I told you true: and yet, dear lady,
Rating myself at nothing, you shall see
How much I was a braggart:.When I told you
My state was nothing, I should then have told you
That I was worse than nothing; for, indeed,
I have engaged myself to a dear friend,
Engaged my friend to his meer enemy,
To feed by means.
                       Shakspeare.

7. O, you are sick of self-love, *Malvolio,* and taste with a distempered appetite: to be generous, guiltless, and of free disposition, is to take those things for bird-bolts, that you deem cannon-bullets. There is no slander in an allowed fool, though he do nothing but rail; nor no railing in a known discreet man, though he do nothing but reprove.
                       Shakspeare.

8.   Her natural posture?—
Chide me, dear stone; that I may say, indeed,
Thou art *Hermione*: or, rather, thou art she,
In thy not chiding; for she was as tender
As infancy and grace. But yet, Paulina,
Hermione was not so much wrinkled; nothing
So aged as this seems.
                       Shakspeare.

9. Yes, *Helen*, you might be my daughter-in-law;
   God shield you mean it not! daughter, and
      mother,
   So strive upon your pulse: What, pale again?
   My fear hath catched your fondness: Now I see
   The mystery of your loneliness, and find
   Your salt tears head. Now to all sense 'tis gross,
   You love my son; invention is ashamed,
   Against the proclamation of thy passion,
   To say, thou dost not: therefore tell me true;
   But tell me then, 'tis so:—for, look, thy cheeks
   Confess it one to the other; and thine eyes
   See it so grossly shown in thy behaviours,
   That in their kind they speak it; only sin
   And hellish obstinacy tie thy tongue,
   That truth should be suspected: Speak is't so?
   If it be so, you have wound a goodly clue;
   If it be not, forswear't: howe'er I charge thee,
   As heaven shall work in me for thine avail,
   To tell me truly.

Shakspeare.

10. Fare thee well; and God have mercy upon one of our souls! He may have mercy upon mine; but my hope is better, and so look to thyself. Thy friend, as thou usest him, and thy sworn enemy, *Andrew Ague-cheek.*

Shakspeare.

11. Hark, *Perdita,*——
   I'll hear you by and by.

Shakspeare.

12. Orsino, noble sir,
    Be pleased that I shake off these names you gave me;
    Antonio never yet was thief, or pirate,
    Though I confess, on base and ground enough,
    Orsino's enemy.   A witchcraft drew me hither:
    That most ungrateful boy there, by your side,
    From the rude sea's enraged and foamy mouth
    Did I redeem; a wreck past hope he was:
    His life I gave him, and did thereto add
    My love, without retention, or restraint,
    All his in dedication: for his sake
    Did I expose myself, pure for his love,
    Into the danger of this adverse town;
    Drew to defend him, when he was beset:
    Where being apprehended, his false cunning
    (Not meaning to partake with me in danger)
    Taught him to face me out of his acquaintance,
    And grew a twenty-years removed thing,
    While one would wink; denied me mine own purse,
    Which I had recommended to his use
    Not half an hour before.
                              Shakspeare.

13. Dost thou hear, *Camillo?*
    I conjure thee, by all the parts of man,
    Which honour does acknowledge,—whereof the least
    Is not this suit of mine,—that thou declare
    What incidency thou dost guess of harm
    Is creeping toward me; how far off, how near;
    Which way to be prevented, if to be;
    If not, how best to bear it.
                              Shakspeare.

200   𝕿𝖍𝖊 𝕷𝖆𝖉𝖞'𝖘 𝕺𝖗𝖆𝖈𝖑𝖊.

14. The king hath happily received, *Macbeth*,
The news of thy success; and when he reads
Thy personal venture in the rebel's fight,
His wonders and his praises do contend,
Which should be thine, or his: Silenced with that,
In viewing o'er the rest o' the selfsame day,
He finds thee in the stout Norweyan ranks,
Nothing afraid of what thyself didst make,
Strange images of death. As thick as tale,
Came post with post; and every one did bear
Thy praises in his kingdom's great defence,
And poured them down before him.
                                        Shakspeare.

15. Come hither, *Hubert.* O my gentle Hubert,
We owe thee much; within this wall of flesh
There is a soul counts thee her creditor,
And with advantage means to pay thy love:
And, my good friend, thy voluntary oath
Lives in this bosom, dearly cherished.
Give me thy hand. I had a thing to say,—
But I will fit it with some better time.
By heaven, Hubert, I am almost ashamed
To say what good respect I have of thee.
                                        Shakspeare.

16. Old *John of Gaunt*, time-honoured Lancaster,
Hast thou, according to thy oath and band,
Brought hither Henry Hereford, thy bold son;
Here to make good the boisterous late appeal,
Which then our leisure would not let us hear,
Against the duke of Norfolk, Thomas Mowbray?
                                        Shakspeare.

17. See, see, *King Richard* doth himself appear,
As doth the blushing discontented sun
From out the fiery portal of the east;
When he perceives, the envious clouds are bent
To dim his glory, and to stain the tract
Of his bright passage to the occident.
Yet looks he like a king; behold, his eye,
As bright as is the eagle's, lightens forth
Controlling majesty: Alack, alack, for wo,
That any harm should stain so fair a show!
Shakspeare.

18. The archdeacon hath divided it
Into three limits, very equally:
England, from Trent and Severn hitherto,
By south and east, is to my part assigned:
All westward, Wales beyond the Severn shore,
And all the fertile land within that bound,
To *Owen Glendower:*—and, dear coz, to you
The remnant northward, lying off from Trent.
And our indentures tripartite are drawn:
Which being sealed interchangeably,
(A business that this night may execute,)
To-morrow, cousin Percy, you, and I,
And my good lord of Worcester, will set forth,
To meet your father, and the Scottish power,
As is appointed us, at Shrewsbury.
My father Glendower is not ready yet,
Nor shall we need his help these fourteen days:—
Within that space you may have drawn together
Your tenants, friends, and neighbouring gentlemen.
Shakspeare.

19. My name is *Constance*; I was Geffrey's wife;
Young Arthur is my son, and he is lost:
I am not mad;—I would to heaven I were!
For then, 'tis like I should forget myself:
Oh, if I could, what grief should I forget!—
Preach some philosophy to make me mad,
And thou shalt be canonized, cardinal;
For, being not mad, but sensible of grief,
My reasonable part produces reason
How I may be delivered of these woes,
And teaches me to kill or hang myself:
If I were mad, I should forget my son;
Or madly think, a babe of clouts were he;
I am not mad; too well, too well I feel
The different plague of each calamity.
Shakspeare.

20.   Why, then I see
A very valiant rebel of that name.
I am the *Prince of Wales;* and think not, Percy,
To share with me in glory any more:
Two stars keep not their motion in one sphere;
Nor can one England brook a double reign,
Of Harry Percy, and the Prince of Wales.
Shakspeare.

21. That *Julius Cæsar* was a famous man;
With what his valour did enrich his wit,
His wit set down to make his valour live:
Death makes no conquest of this conqueror;
For now he lives in fame, though not in life.
Shakspeare.

22. Then, as I said, the duke, great *Bolingbroke*,
Mounted upon a hot and fiery steed,
Which his aspiring rider seem'd to know,—
With slow, but stately pace kept on his course,
While all tongues cried—God save thee, Boling-
broke!
You would have thought the very windows spake,
So many greedy looks of young and old
Through casements darted their desiring eyes
Upon his visage; and that all the walls,
With painted imagery, had said at once,—
Jesu preserve thee! welcome, Bolingbroke!
Whilst he, from one side to the other turning,
Bare-headed, lower than his proud steed's neck,
Bespake them thus,—I thank you, countrymen:
And thus still doing, thus he passed along.
                                    Shakspeare.

23.   Too modest are you;
More cruel to your good report, than grateful
To us that give you truly: by your patience,
If 'gainst yourself you be incensed, we'll put you
(Like one that means his proper harm) in manacles,
Then reason safely with you. Therefore be it known,
As to us, to all the world, that Caius Marcius
Wears this war's garland: in token of the which,
My noble steed, known to the camp, I give him,
With all his trim belonging; and, from this time,
For what he did before Corioli, call him,
With all the applause and clamour of the host,
Caius Marcius Coriolanus.——
Bear the addition nobly ever!
                                    Shakspeare.

24. A goodly portly man, i'faith, and a corpulent;
of a cheerful look, a pleasing eye, and a most noble
carriage: and, as I think, his age some fifty, or, by'r-
Lady, inclining to threescore; and now I remember
me, his name is *Falstaff*: if that man should bé lewdly
given, he deceiveth me; for, Harry, I see virtue in his
looks. If then the fruit may be known by the tree, as
the tree by the fruit, then, peremptorily I speak it,
there is virtue in that Falstaff: him keep with, the rest
banish. And tell me now, thou naughty varlet, tell
me, where hast thou been this month?

Shakspeare.

25. *Brutus*, I do observe you now of late;
　　I have not from your eyes that gentleness,
　　And show of love, as I was wont to have.
　　You bear too stubborn and too strange a hand
　　Over your friend that loves you.

Shakspeare.

26. Thus stands my state, 'twixt *Cade* and York dis-
　　　　tressed;
　　Like to a ship, that, having 'scaped a tempest,
　　Is straightway calmed, and boarded with a pirate·
　　But now is Cade driven back, his men dispersed;
　　And now is York in arms, to second him.——
　　I pray thee, Buckingham, go and meet him;
　　And ask him, what's the reason of these arms.
　　Tell him, I'll send duke Edmund to the Tower:—
　　And, Somerset, we will commit thee thither,
　　Until his army be dismissed from him.

Shakspeare.

27.   Leave me awhile.—
It shall be to the duchess of Alençon,
The French king's sister: he shall marry her.—
Anne Bullen! No; I'll no Anne Bullens for him:
There's more in't than fair visage.—Bullen!
No, we'll no Bullens!—Speedily I wish
To hear from Rome.—The marchioness of Penr
    broke!
                                    Shakspeare.

28. Well, well, he was the covertest sheltered traitor
That ever lived.——Look you, my lord mayor,
Would you imagine, or almost believe,
(Were't not, that by great preservation
We live to tell it you) the subtle traitor
This day had plotted, in the council-house,
To murder me, and my good lord of *Gloster?*
                                    Shakspeare.

29.   *Cassius,*
    Be not deceived: If I have veiled my look,
I turn the trouble of my countenance
Merely upon myself. ' Vexed I am
Of late with passions of some difference,
Conceptions only proper to myself,
Which give some soil, perhaps, to my behaviours:
But let not therefore my good friends be grieved,
(Among which number, Cassius, be you one,)
Nor construe any further my neglect,
Than that poor Brutus, with himself at war,
Forgets the shows of love to other men.
                                    Shakspeare.

30. Speak to me home, mince not the general tongue:
Name *Cleopatra* as she's called in Rome:
Rail thou in Fulvia's phrase; and taunt my faults
With such full license, as both truth and malice
Have power to utter. O, then we bring forth weeds,
When our quick winds lie still; and our ill, told us,
Is as our earing. Fare thee well awhile.

Shakspeare.

31. *Scribe.* Say, *Katharine, Queen of England,* come
into the court.

Crier. Katharine, queen of England, &c.

[*The Queen makes no answer, rises out of her chair,
goes about the court, comes to the king, and kneels at his
feet; then speaks.*]

Queen. Sir, I desire you, do me right and justice;
And to bestow your pity on me: for
I am a most poor woman, and a stranger,
Born out of your dominions: having here
No judge indifferent, nor no more assurance
Of equal friendship and proceeding. Alas, sir,
In what have I offended you? what cause
Hath my behaviour given to your displeasure,
That thus you should proceed to put me off,
And take your good grace from me? Heaven
witness,
I have been to you a true and humble wife,
At all times to your will conformable:
Ever in fear to kindle your dislike,
Yea, subject to your countenance; glad, or sorry,
As I saw it inclined. When was the hour
I ever contradicted your desire,

Or made it not mine too? Or which of your
    friends
Have I not strove to love, although I knew
He were mine enemy? what friend of mine,
That had to him derived your anger, did I
Continue in my liking? nay, gave not notice
He was from thence discharged? Sir, call to mind,
That I have been your wife, in this obedience,
Upwards of twenty years, and have been blest
With many children by you: If, in the course
And process of this time, you can report,
And prove it too, against mine honour aught,
My bond to wedlock, or my love and duty
Against your sacred person, in God's name,
Turn me away; and let the foulest contempt
Shut door upon me, and so give me up
To the sharpest kind of justice. Please you, sir,
The king, your father, was reputed for
A prince most prudent, of an excellent
And unmatched wit and judgment: Ferdinand,
My father, king of Spain, was reckoned one
The wisest prince, that there had reigned by many
A year before: It is not to be questioned
That they had gathered a wise council to them
Of every realm, that did debate this business,
Who deemed our marriage lawful; Wherefore
    humbly
Beseech you, sir, to spare me, till I may
Be by my friends in Spain advised; whose counsel
I will implore: If not; i' the name of God,
Your pleasure be fulfilled!

Shakspeare.

32.   *Wolsey.* Cromwell, I did not think to shed a tear
       In all my miseries; but thou hast forced me,
       Out of thy honest truth, to play the woman.
       Let's dry our eyes: And thus far hear me, Cromwell;
       And,—when I am forgotten, as I shall be;
       And sleep in dull cold marble, where no mention
       Of me more must be heard of,—say, I taught thee,
       Say, *Wolsey,*—that once trod the ways of glory,
       And sounded all the depths and shoals of honour,—
       Found thee a way out of his wreck to rise in;
       A sure and safe one, though thy master missed it.
       Mark but my fall, and that that ruined me.
       Cromwell, I charge thee, fling away ambition;
       By that sin fell the angels; how can man, then,
       The image of his Maker, hope to win by 't?
       Love thyself last: cherish those hearts that hate thee;
       Corruption wins not more than honesty.
       Still in thy right hand carry gentle peace,
       To silence envious tongues.   Be just, and fear not:
       Let all the ends thou aimest at be thy country's,
       Thy God's, and truth's; then if thou fallest, O
              Cromwell,
       Thou fallest a blessed martyr.   Serve the king;
       And,—Pr'ythee, lead me in:
       There take an inventory of all I have,
       To the last penny; 'tis the king's: my robe,
       And my integrity to heaven, is all
       I dare now call mine own. O Cromwell, Cromwell,
       Had I but served my God with half the zeal
       I served my king, He would not in mine age
       Have left me naked to mine enemies.
                                          Shakspeare.

33.   *Brutus.* Another general shout!
I do believe, that these applauses are
For some new honours that are heaped on *Cæsar.*
   Cas. Why, man, he doth bestride the narrow
      world
Like a Colossus; and we petty men
Walk under his huge legs and peep about
To find ourselves dishonourable graves.
Men at some time are masters of their fates:
The fault, dear Brutus, is not in our stars,
But in ourselves, that we are underlings.
Brutus, and Cæsar: What should be in that Cæsar?
Why should that name be sounded more than yours?
Write them together, yours is as fair a name;
Sound them, it doth become the mouth as well:
Weigh them, it is as heavy; conjure with them,
Brutus will start a spirit as soon as Cæsar.
Now, in the names of all the gods at once,
Upon what meat doth this our Cæsar feed,
That he is grown so great?   Age, thou art shamed;
Rome, thou hast lost the breed of noble bloods!
When went there by an age, since the great flood,
But it was famed with more than with one man?
When could they say, till now, that talked of Rome,
That her wide walls encompassed but one man?
Now is it Rome indeed, and room enough,
When there is in it but one only man.
O! you and I have heard our fathers say,
There was a Brutus once that would have brooked
The eternal devil to keep his state in Rome,
As easily as a king.
                              Shakspeare.
14

34.   *War.* The bloody parliament shall this be called,
Unless *Plantagenet*, duke of York, be king;
And bashful Henry deposed, whose cowardice
Hath made us by-words to our enemies.
    York. Then leave me not, my lords; be resolute;
I mean to take possession of my right.
    War. Neither the king, nor he that loves him best,
The proudest he that holds up Lancaster,
Dares stir a wing, if Warwick shake his bells.
I'll plant Plantagenet, root him up who dares:—
Resolve thee, Richard; claim the English crown.
                      Shakspeare.

35.   Most noble *Antony,*
Let not the piece of virtue, which is set
Betwixt us, as the cement of our love,
To keep it builded, be the ram, to batter
The fortress of it: for better might we
Have loved without this mean, if on both parts
This be not cherished.
                      Shakspeare.

36.   Up to the eastern tower,
Whose height commands as subject all the vale,
To see the battle. *Hector,* whose patience
Is, as a virtue, fixed, to-day was moved;
He chid Andromache, and struck his armourer;
And, like as there were husbandry in war,
Before the sun rose, he was harnessed light,
And to the field goes he; where every flower
Did, as a prophet, weep what it foresaw
In Hector's wrath.
                      Shakspeare.

37. Hail to thee, worthy *Timon;*—and to all,
  That of his bounties taste!—The five best senses
  Acknowledge thee their patron; and come freely
  To gratulate thy plenteous bosom;
  The ear, taste, touch, smell, pleased from thy table
      rise;
  They only now come but to feast thine eyes.
  Shakspeare.

38. Thrift, thrift, *Horatio!* The funeral baked meats
  Did coldly furnish forth the marriage tables.
  'Would I had met my dearest foe in heaven,
  Or ever I had seen that day, Horatio!——
  My father,—Methinks, I see my father.
  Shakspeare.

39.   For the Roman eagle,
  From south to west on wing soaring aloft,
  Lessened herself, and in the beams o' the sun
  So vanished: which foreshowed, our princely eagle,
  The imperial Cæsar, should again unite
  His favour with the radiant *Cymbeline,*
  Which shines here in the west.
  Shakspeare.

40. A sovereign shame so elbows him: his own un-
      kindness,
  That stripped her from his benediction, turned her
  To foreign casualties, gave her dear rights
  To his dog-hearted daughters,—these things sting
  His mind so venomously, that burning shame
  Detains him from *Cordelia.*
  Shakspeare.

41.　　*Rom*. He jests at scars, that never felt a wound.—
　　　　But soft! what light through yonder window breaks?
　　　　It is the east, and *Juliet* is the sun!—
　　　　　　　　　　[*Juliet appears above at a window.*
　　　　Arise, fair sun, and kill the envious moon,
　　　　Who is already sick and pale with grief,
　　　　That thou her maid art far more fair than she:
　　　　Be not her maid, since she is envious;
　　　　Her vestal livery is but sick and green,
　　　　And none but fools do wear it: cast it off.—
　　　　It is my lady: Oh, it is my love:
　　　　Oh, that she knew she were!——
　　　　She speaks, yet she says nothing: What of that?
　　　　Her eye discourses, I will answer it.——
　　　　I am too bold, 'tis not to me it speaks:
　　　　Two of the fairest stars in all the heaven,
　　　　Having some business, do entreat her eyes
　　　　To twinkle in their spheres till they return.
　　　　What if her eyes were there, they in her head?
　　　　The brightness of her cheek would shame those stars,
　　　　As daylight doth a lamp: her eye in heaven
　　　　Would through the airy region stream so bright,
　　　　That birds would sing, and think it were not night.
　　　　See, how she leans her cheek upon her hand!
　　　　Oh, that I were a glove upon that hand,
　　　　That I might touch that cheek!
　　　　　　　　　　　　　　　　Shakspeare.

42. Valiant *Othello*, we must straight employ you
　　　Against the general enemy Ottoman.—
　　　I did not see you; welcome, gentle signior;
　　　We lacked your counsel and your help to-night.
　　　　　　　　　　　　　　　　Shakspeare.

43. Words, vows, gifts, tears, and love's full sacrifice,
He offers in another's enterprise:
But more in Troilus thousand fold I see
Than in the glass of Pandar's praise may be.
                                    \ *Shakspeare.*

44. *Juliet.* O *Romeo, Romeo!* wherefore art thou
    Romeo?
Deny thy father, and refuse thy name;
Or, if thou wilt not, be but sworn my love,
And I'll no longer be a Capulet.
    Rom. Shall I hear more, or shall I speak at this?
                                    [*Aside.*
    Jul. 'Tis but thy name that is my enemy;
Thou art thyself, though not a Montague.
What's Montague? it is nor hand, nor foot,
Nor arm, nor face, nor any other part:
What's in a name? That which we call a rose,
By any other name would smell as sweet;
So Romeo would, were he not Romeo called,
Retain that dear perfection which he owes,
Without that title:—Romeo, doff thy name;
And for that name, which is no part of thee,
Take all myself.
                                    Shakspeare.

45. Good *Hamlet,* cast thy nighted colour off,
And let thine eye look like a friend on Denmark.
Do not, for ever, with thy veiled lids
Seek for thy noble father in the dust:
Thou knowest, 'tis common: all, that live, must die,
Passing through nature to eternity.
                                    Shakspeare.

46.   O most small fault,
How ugly didst thou in Cordelia show!
Which, like an engine, wrenched by frame of nature
From the fixt place, drew from my heart all love,
And added to the gall.   O *Lear, Lear, Lear!*
Beat at this gate, that let thy folly in,
And thy dear judgment out!—Go, go, my people.
                               Shakspeare.

47. Fear it, *Ophelia,* fear it, my dear sister;
And keep you in the rear of your affection,
Out of the shot and danger of desire.
The chariest maid is prodigal enough,
If she unmask her beauty to the moon:
Virtue itself scapes not calumnious strokes:
The canker galls the infants of the spring
Too oft before their buttons be disclosed;
And in the morn and liquid dew of youth
Contagious blastments are most imminent.
Be wary, then: best safety lies in fear;
Youth to itself rebels, though none else near.
                               Shakspeare.

48.   These things to hear,
Would *Desdemona* seriously incline:
But still the house affairs would draw her thence;
Which ever as she could with haste despatch,
She'd come again, and with a greedy ear
Devour up my discourse: Which I observing,
Took once a pliant hour; and found good means
To draw from her a prayer of earnest heart,
That I would all my pilgrimage dilate,

Whereof by parcels she had something heard,
But not intentively: I did consent;
And often did beguile her of her tears,
When I did speak of some distressful stroke
That my youth suffered. My story being done,
She gave me for my pains a world of sighs:
She swore,—In faith, 'twas strange, 'twas passing
    strange;
'Twas pitiful, 'twas wondrous pitiful:
She wished she had not heard it; yet she wished
That heaven had made her such a man: she thanked
    me;
And bade me, if I had a friend that loved her,
I should but teach him how to tell my story,
And that would woo her. Upon this hint, I spake:
She loved me for the dangers I had past;
And I loved her that she did pity them.
This only is the witchcraft I have used;
Here comes the lady, let her witness it.
                     Shakspeare.

49.   *Pol.* Yet here, *Laertes!* aboard, aboard, for shame;
The wind sits in the shoulder of your sail,
And you are stayed for: There,—my blessings with
    you;   [*Laying his hands on Laertes' head.*
And these few precepts in thy memory:
Look thou character. Give thy thoughts no tongue,
Nor any unproportioned thought his act.
Be thou familiar, but by no means vulgar.
The friends thou hast, and their adoption tried,
Grapple them to thy soul with hooks of steel;
But do not dull thy palm with entertainment

Of each new-hatched, unfledged comrade.   Beware
Of entrance to a quarrel; but, being in,
Bear it that the opposer may beware of thee.
Give every man thine ear, but few thy voice:
Take each man's censure, but reserve thy judgment.
Costly thy habit as thy purse can buy,
But not expressed in fancy; rich, not gaudy:
For the apparel oft proclaims the man;
And they in France, of the best rank and station,
Are most select, and generous chief in that.
Neither a borrower nor a lender be:
For loan oft loses both itself and friend;
And borrowing dulls the edge of husbandry.
This above all,—To thine ownself be true;
And it must follow, as the night the day,
Thou canst not then be false to any man.
Farewell: my blessing season this in thee!

Shakspeare.

50. 'Tis one *Iago*, ancient to the general.

Shakspeare.

Which is your favourite Historical Character?

ITH that most fatal field, I will not here begin
Where *Norman William,* first the Conqueror,
   did win
The day at Hastings, where the valiant Harold
   slain,
Resigned his crown, whose soil the colour
   doth retain
Of the English blood there shed, as the earth
   still kept the scar:
Which since not ours begot, but an invasive
   war,
Among our home-fought fields, hath no de-
   scription here.
                              Drayton.

2. The battle of Blore-heath, the place doth next supply,
'Twixt *Richard Nevil,* that great earl of Salisbury,
Who, with the duke of York, had at Saint Alban's late,
That glorious battle got with uncontrolled fate.
                              Drayton.

3. I choose the battle next of Shrewsbury to chant,
    Betwixt Henry the Fourth, the son of John of Gaunt,
    And the stout Perciies, *Henry Hotspur* and his eame
    The earl of Wor'ster, who the rightful diadem
    Had from king Richard reft, and heaved up to his seat
    This Henry whom (too soon) they found to be too
        great,
    Him seeking to depose, and to the rule prefer
    Richard's proclaimed heir, their cousin Mortimer,
    Whom Owen Glendour then in Wales a prisoner
        stayed,
    Whom to their part they won, and thus their plot
        they laid,
    That Glendour should have Wales, as long as Severn
        went,
    The Percies all the north, that lay beyond the Trent;
    And Mortimer from thence the south to be his share;
    Which Henry having heard, doth for the war prepare,
    And down to Cheshire makes (where gathering
        powers they were)
    At Shrewsbury to meet, and doth affront them there:
    With him his peerless son, the princely Henry, came,
    With the earl of Stafford, and of gentlemen of name,
    Blunt, Shyrley, Clifton, men that very powerful were,
    With Cockayne, Calverly, Massy, and Mortimer,
    Gausell, and Wendsley, all in friends and tenants
        strong,
    Resorting to the king still as he passed along;
    Which in the open field before the ranged fights,
    He, with his warlike son, there dubbed his maiden
        knights.

                                        Drayton.

4. 'Twas after dread Pultowa's day,
   When fortune left the *Royal Swede*,
Around a slaughtered army lay,
   No more to combat and to bleed.
The power and glory of the war,
   Faithless as their vain votaries, men,
Had passed to the triumphant Czar,
   And Moscow's walls were safe again,
Until a day more dark and drear,
And a more memorable year,
Should give to slaughter and to shame
A mightier host and haughtier name;
A greater wreck, a deeper fall,
A shock to one—a thunderbolt to all.

Byron.

5.   What were we,
If *Brutus* had not lived? He died in giving
Rome liberty, but left a deathless lesson—
A name which is a virtue, and a soul
Which multiplies itself throughout all time,
When wicked men wax mighty, and a state
Turns servile: he and his high friend were styled
"The last of Romans!"

Byron.

6.   I will not see
The blood of Nimrod and *Semiramis*
Sink in the earth, and thirteen hundred years
Of empire ending like a shepherd's tale;
He must be roused.

Byron.

7. And all are fellows in their need.
   Among the rest, *Mazeppa* made
   His pillow in an old oak's shade—
   Himself as rough, and scarce less old,
   The Ukraine's hetman, calm and bold;
   But first, outspent with this long course,
   The Cossack prince rubbed down his horse,
   And made for him a leafy bed,
   And smoothed his fetlocks and his mane,
   And slacked his girth, and stripped his rein,
   And joyed to see how well he fed.
                                    Byron.

8. *Doge Dandolo* survived to ninety summers
   To vanquish empires and refuse their crown;
   I will resign a crown, and make the state
   Renew its freedom—but oh! by what means?
   The noble end must justify them—What
   Are a few drops of human blood? 'tis false,
   The blood of tyrants is not human? they,
   Like to incarnate Molochs, feed on ours,
   Until 'tis time to give them to the tombs
   Which they have made so populous.—Oh world!
   Oh men! what are ye, and our best designs,
   That we must work by crime to punish crime?
   And slay as if Death had but this one gate,
   When a few years would make the sword super-
              fluous;
   And I, upon the verge of the unknown realm,
   Yet send so many heralds on before me?—
   I must not ponder this.
                                    Byron.

9. Our fathers did not fly from *Attila*
   Into these isles, where palaces have sprung
   On banks redeemed from the rude ocean's ooze,
   To own a thousand despots in his place.
   Better bow down before the Hun, and call
   A Tartar lord, than these swoln silk-worms masters;
   The first at least was man, and used his sword
   As sceptre: these unmanly creeping things
   Command our swords, and rule us with a word
   As with a spell.

   Byron.

10. The reason's obvious: if there's an éclat,
    They lose their caste at once, as do the Parias,
    And when the delicacies of the law
    Have filled their papers with their comments
    various,
    Society, that china without flaw,
    (The hypocrite!) will banish them like *Marius*,
    To sit amidst the ruins of their guilt:
    For Fame's a Carthage not so soon rebuilt.

    Byron.

11. And since "there's safety in a multitude
    Of counsellors," as *Solomon* has said,
    Or some one for him, in some sage grave mood:—
    Indeed we see the daily proof displayed
    In senates, at the bar, in wordy feud,
    Where'er collective wisdom can parade,
    Which is the only cause that we can guess
    Of Britain's present wealth and happiness.

    Byron.

12. And therefore what I throw off is ideal—
     Lowered, leavened, like a history of Freemasons;
Which bears the same relation to the real,
     As Captain Parry's voyage may do to *Jason's*.
The grand Arcanum's not for men to see all;
     My music has some mystic diapasons;
And there is much which could not be appreciated
In any manner by the uninitiated.
Byron.

13. When I prepared my bark first to obey,
     As it should still obey, the helm, my mind,
And carry prose or rhyme, and this my lay
     Of *Charles the Emperor*, whom you will find
By several pens already praised; but they
     Who to diffuse his glory were inclined,
For all that I can see in prose or verse,
Have understood Charles badly—and wrote worse.
Byron.

14. Oh, thou wouldst have me doubtless set up edicts—
"Obey the king—contribute to his treasure—
Recruit his phalanx—spill your blood at bidding—
Fall down and worship, or get up and toil."
Or thus—" *Sardanapalus* on this spot
Slew fifty thousand of his enemies.
These are their sepulchres, and this his trophy."
I leave such things to conquerors; enough
For me, if I can make my subjects feel
The weight of human misery less, and glide
Ungroaning to the tomb; I take no license
Which I deny to them. We all are men.
Byron.

15. Twelve paladins had Charles, in court, of whom
　　The wisest and most famous was *Orlando;*
Him traitor Gan conducted to the tomb
　　In Roncesvalles, as the villain planned too,
While the horn rang so loud, and knelled the doom
　　Of their sad rout, though he did all knight can do,
And Dante in his comedy has given
To him a happy seat with Charles in heaven.
　　　　　　　　　　　　　　　Byron.

16. France hath twice too well been taught
The "moral lesson" dearly bought—
Her safety sits not on a throne,
With Capet or *Napoleon!*
But in equal rights and laws,
Hearts and hands in one great cause—
Freedom, such as God hath given
Unto all beneath his heaven,
With their breath, and from their birth,
Though guilt would sweep it from the earth;
With a fierce and lavish hand .
Scattering nations' wealth like sand;
. Pouring nations' blood like water,
In imperial seas of slaughter!
　　　　　　　　　　　　　　　Byron.

17. Survey the globe, each ruder realm explore;
From Reason's faintest ray to *Newton* soar.
What different spheres to human bliss assigned!
What slow gradations in the scale of mind!
Yet mark in each these mystic wonders wrought;
Oh mark the sleepless energies of thought!
　　　　　　　　　　　　　　　Rogers.

18. *Columbus* erred not.   In that awful hour,
Sent forth to save, and girt with God-like power,
And glorious as the regent of the sun,
An angel came!   He spoke, and it was done!
He spoke, and, at his call, a mighty wind,
Not like the fitful blast, with fury blind,
But deep, majestic, in its destined course,
Sprung with unerring, unrelenting force,
From the bright East.   Tides duly ebbed and flowed;
Stars rose and set; and new horizons glowed;
Yet still it blew!   As with primeval sway
Still did its ample spirit, night and day,
Move on the waters!—All, resigned to Fate,
Folded their arms and sate; and seemed to wait
Some sudden change; and sought, in chill suspense,
New spheres of being, and new modes of sense;
As men departing, though not doomed to die,
And midway on their passage to eternity.

Rogers.

19. On through that gate misnamed, through which
     before
Went Sidney, Russell, Raleigh, Cranmer, More,
On into twilight within walls of stone,
Then to the place of trial; and alone.
Alone before his judges in array
Stands for his life· there, on that awful day,
Counsel of friends—all human help denied—
All but from her who sits the pen to guide,
Like that sweet saint who sate by *Russell's* side
Under the judgment-seat.

Rogers.

20.   As now at Virgil's tomb
We bless the shade, and bid the verdure bloom:
So *Tully* paused, amid the wrecks of Time,
On the rude stone to trace the truth sublime;
When at his feet, in honoured dust disclosed,
The immortal Sage of Syracuse reposed.
And as he long in sweet delusion hung,
Where once a Plato taught, a Pindar sung;
Who now but meets him musing, when he roves
His ruined Tusculan's romantic groves?
In Rome's great forum, who but hears him roll
His moral thunders o'er the subject soul?
                                        Rogers.

21. *Nelson* was once Britannia's god of war,
        And still should be so, but the tide is turned;
There's no more to be said of Trafalgar,
        'Tis with our hero quietly inurned;
Because the army's grown more popular,
        At which the naval people are concerned:
Besides, the prince is all for the land-service,
Forgetting Duncan, Nelson, Howe, and Jervis.
                                        Byron.

22. Ask not if courts or camps dissolve the charm:
Say why *Vespasian* loved his Sabine farm;
Why great Navarre, when France and freedom bled
Sought the lone limits of a forest-shed.
When Diocletian's self-corrected mind
The imperial fasces of a world resigned,
Say why we trace the labours of his spade,
In calm Salona's philosophic shade.
                                        Rogers.

15

23. And now behold him in an evil day
    Serving the state again—not as before,
    Not foot to foot, the war-whoop at his door,—
    But in the Senate; and (though round him fly
    The jest, the sneer, the subtle sophistry,)
    With honest dignity, with manly sense,
    And every charm of natural eloquence,
    Like *Hampden* struggling in his country's cause,
    The first, the foremost to obey the laws,
    The last to brook oppression. On he moves,
    Careless of blame while his own heart approves,
    Careless of ruin—("For the general good
    'Tis not the first time I shall shed my blood.")
                         Rogers.

24. And thou, dread statue! yet existent in
    The austerest form of naked majesty,
    Thou who beheldest, mid the assassins' din,
    At thy bathed base the bloody Cæsar lie,
    Folding his robe in dying dignity,
    An offering to thine altar from the queen
    Of gods and men, great Nemesis, did he die?
    And thou, too, perish, *Pompey?* have ye been
    Victors of countless kings, or puppets of a scene?
                         Byron.

25. Luctatius, who the good luck had to end
    Rome's first great Punic war, did on the land
    By practice teach his seamen how to mend
    That discipline in peace by which wars stand;
    As *Philopœmen* made Achaia spread
    By lazy peace, yet lively governed.
                         Lord Brooke.

26. Oh! she was good as she was fair.
    None—none on earth above her!
    As pure in thought as angels are,
    To know her was to love her.
    When little, and her eyes, her voice,
    Her every gesture said "rejoice,"
    Her coming was a gladness;
    And, as she grew, her modest grace,
    Her downcast look 'twas heaven to trace,
    When, shading with her hand her face,
    She half inclined to sadness.
    Her voice, whate'er she said, enchanted;
    Like music to the heart it went.
    And her dark eyes—how eloquent!
    Ask what they would, 'twas granted.
    Her father loved her as his fame;
    —And *Bayard's* self had done the same!
                                        Rogers.

27. Such as she did at Allia of old,
    When naked Gauls both took and burnt the town
    Or Italy from *Spartacus* the bold;
    When by a slave their eagles were thrown down,
    So that the monarch fell by outward fate,
    Whereas the people's own faults shak't their state.
                                        Brooke.

28. Indeede I finde, within this glasse of mine,
    Justinian, that proude vngrateful prince,
    Which made to begge, bold *Belisarius*
    His trustie man, which had so stoutly fought
    In his defence, with eury enimy.
                                        Gascoigne.

29. Up rose St. Pierre, when morning shone;
    —And Jacqueline, his child, was gone!
    Oh what the maddening thought that came?
    Dishonour coupled with his name!
    By Condé at Rocroi he stood;
    By Turenne, when the Rhine ran blood.
    Two banners of Castile he gave
    Aloft in Notre Dame to wave;
    Nor did thy cross, *St. Louis*, rest
    Upon a purer, nobler breast.
                              Rogers.

30. Grey, thou hast served, and well, the sacred cause
    That Hampden, *Sidney* died for. Thou hast stood,
    Scorning all thought of self, from first to last,
    Among the foremost in that glorious field;
    From first to last; and, ardent as thou art,
    Held on with equal step as best became
    A lofty mind, loftiest when most assailed;
    Never, though galled by many a barbed shaft,
    By many a bitter taunt from friend and foe,
    Swerving, nor shrinking.   •
                              Rogers.

31. As *Constantine the Great*, that godly emperor,
    Here first the Christian church that did to peace
              restore,
    Whose ever-blessed birth (as by the power divine)
    The Roman empire brought into the British line,
    Constantinople's crown, and the ancient Britons'
              glory.
    So other here, we have to finish up our story.
                              Drayton.

32. Whoe'er thou art, approach, and, with a sigh,
Mark where the small remains of greatness lie.
There sleeps the dust of *Fox* for ever gone;
How near the place where late his glory shone!
And, though no more ascends the voice of prayer,
Though the last footsteps cease to linger there,
Still, like an awful dream that comes again,
Alas, at best, as transient and as vain,
Still do I see (while through the vaults of night
The funeral-song once more proclaims the rite)
The moving pomp along the shadowy aisle,
That, like a darkness, filled the solemn pile;
The illustrious line, that in long order led,
Of those that loved him living, mourned him
    dead;
Of those the few, that for their country stood
Round him who dared be singularly good;
All, of all ranks, that claimed him for their own;
And nothing wanting—but himself alone!
                                    Rogers.

33. *Sylla* was first of victors; but our own
The sagest of usurpers, Cromwell; he
Too swept off senates while he hewed the throne
Down to a block—immortal rebel! See
What crimes it costs to be a moment free
And famous through all ages! but beneath
His fate the moral lurks of destiny;
His day of double victory and death
Beheld him win two realms, and, happier, yield his
    breath.
                                    Byron.

34. Can tyrants but by tyrants conquered be,
    And freedom find no champion and no child
    Such as Columbia saw arise when she
    Sprung forth a Pallas, armed and undefiled?
    Or must such minds be nourished in the wild,
    Deep in the unpruned forest, midst the roar
    Of cataracts, where nursing Nature smiled
    On infant *Washington?*   Has earth no more
    Such seeds within her breast, or Europe no such
        shore?
                                       Byron.

35. Then turn we to her latest tribune's name,
    From her ten thousand tyrants turn to thee,
    Redeemer of dark centuries of shame—
    The friend of Petrarch—hope of Italy—
    Rienzi! last of Romans!   While the tree
    Of freedom's withered trunk puts forth a leaf,
    Even for thy tomb a garland let it be—
    The forum's champion, and the people's chief—
    Her new-born Numa thou—with reign, alas! too
        brief.
                                       Byron.

36. On these states, what true judgment can we lay
    Which by the arts of crafty tyranny,
    So to their ends do people's humours sway,
    As thrones right grow a kind of mystery?
    Whence *Mahomet* himself an idol makes,
    And draws mankind to Mecha for his sake.
                                       Brooke.

37. When riseth Lacedemon's hardihood,
  When Thebes *Epaminondas* rears again,
  When Athens' children are with hearts endued,
  When Grecian mothers shall give birth to men,
  Then mayst thou be restored; but not till then.
  A thousand years scarce serve to form a state;
  An hour may lay it in the dust; and when
  Can man its shattered splendour renovate,
  Recall its virtues back, and vanquish time and fate?
  Byron.

38. For it is not to them of banishment
  Sufficient ground, to be reputed just?
  What other cause was there of discontent
  'Gainst *Aristides*, but his worth's mistrust?
  How used they him that conquered Marathon?
  Or him who Xerxes' host had overthrown?
  Brooke.

39. What did it profit the great *Charles the Fift*
  To traffic with the proud simplicity
  Of German princes, by unprincely shift,
  Mislettered writs, a conclave subtilty?
  Since ill fate then, and ever did befall
  That broken faith aspirers work withal.
  Brooke.

40. Like *Cromwell's* pranks; but although truth exacts
  These amiable descriptions from the scribes,
  As most essential to their hero's story,
  They do not much contribute to his glory.
  Byron.

41. Of this kind *Solon* was in Athens one;
    Lycurgus cobwebs over Sparta spread;
    The Locrians by Seleucus nets were known,
    By Zoroasters Bactria was misled;
    Numa was he that first enthralled Rome,
    And nature's freedom under legal doom.
                            Brooke.

42. Hence again France, though ever martial bent,
    Was by her late *Fourth Henry's* policy
    Known for a paradise-like continent,
    Who out of that discerned fertility
    Both multiplied the crown, and people's part,
    By nature's emulation with his art.
                            Brooke.

43. *Lewis the Eleventh,* of craft, not majesty,
    The perfect type, being asked what the crown
    Revenues might of France amount to be,
    Said, France a meadow was, which, mow it down
    As oft as need, or pleasure did require,
    Would yet grow up again to feed desire.
                            Brooke.

44. And *Fabius,* surnamed *Maximus,*
    Could ioyne such learning with experience,
    As made his name more famous than the rest.
                         Gascoigne.

45. O that al kings would (*Alexander* like)
    Hold euermore, one finger streight stretcht out,
    To thrust in eyes, of all their master theeues.
                         Gascoigne.

46. They saw at Canterbury the Cathedral;
    Black *Edward's* helm, and Beckett's bloody stone,
    Were pointed out as usual by the bedral,
    In the same quaint, uninterested tone:
    There's glory again for you, gentle reader! all
    Ends in a rusty casque and dubious bone,
    Half-solved into those sodas or magnesias,
    Which form that bitter draught, the human species.
                                    Byron.

47. Among the first,—I will not say the *first*,
    For such precedence upon such occasions
    Will oftentimes make deadly quarrels burst
    Out between friends as well as allied nations;
    The Briton must be bold who really durst
    Put to such trial John Bull's partial patience,
    As say that *Wellington* at Waterloo
    Was beaten,—though the Prussians say so too.
                                    Byron.

48. I am neither Alexander nor Hephæstion,
    Nor ever had for *abstract* fame much passion;
    But would much rather have a sound digestion,
    Than *Bonaparte's* cancer:—could I dash on
    Through fifty victories to shame or fame,
    Without a stomach—what were a good name?
                                    Byron.

49. Her next amusement was more fanciful;
    She smiled at mad *Suwarrow's* rhymes, who threw
    Into a Russian couplet, rather dull,
    The whole gazette of thousands whom he slew.
                                    Byron.

50. And *Scypio*, condemnes the Romaine rule,
    Which suffred him (that had so truely serued)
    To leade pore life, at his (Lynternum) ferme,
    Which did deserue, such worthy recompence.
    Yea herewithal most Souldiours of our time
    Beleeve for truth, that proude Justinian
    Did neuer die, without good store of heyres.
    And Romanes race, cannot be rooted out,
    Such yssence springs, of such vnplesant budds.
                            Gascoigne.

Who is your Favourite Poet?

NOW, seraph-winged, among the stars we soar;
Now distant ages, like a day, explore,
And judge the act, the actor now no more;
Or, in a thankless hour condemned to live,
From others claim what these refuse to give,
And dart, like *Milton*, an unerring eye
Through the dim curtains of Futurity.
Rogers.

2. I saw the sun go down!—Ah, then 'twas thine
Ne'er to forget some volume half divine,
Shakspeare's or *Dryden's*—through the checkered
shade
Borne in thy hand behind thee as we strayed;
And where we sate (and many a halt we made)
To read there with a fervour all thine own,
And in thy grand and melancholy tone,
Some splendid passage not to thee unknown,
Fit theme for long discourse.
Rogers.

3. Can *Virgil's* verse, can Raphael's touch impart
    Those finer features of the feeling heart,
    Those tenderer tints that shun the careless eye,
    And in the world's contagious climate die?

                               Rogers.

4. Nor boast, O Choisy, seat of soft delight,
    The secret charm of thy voluptuous night.
    Vain is the blaze of wealth, the pomp of power!
    Lo, here, attendant on the shadowy hour,
    Thy closet-supper, served by hands unseen,
    Sheds, like an evening-star, its ray serene,
    To hail our coming. Not a step profane
    Dares, with rude sound, the cheerful rite restrain;
    And, while the frugal banquet glows revealed,
    Pure and unbought,—the natives of my field;
    While blushing fruits through scattered leaves
           invite,
    Still clad in bloom, and veiled in azure light;—
    With wine, as rich in years as *Horace* sings,
    With water, clear as his own fountain flings,
    The shifting side-board plays its humbler part,
    Beyond the triumphs of a Loriot's art.

                               Rogers.

5. Plato ('tis true) great *Homer* doth commend,
      Yet from his common-weale did him exile;
    Nor is it words, that doe with words contend,
      Of deeds they vary, and demurre of stile:
    "How to please all, as no words yet could tell;
    So what one act did all yet censure well?"

                              Lord Brooke.

6. Ferrara! in thy wide and grass-grown streets,
   Whose symmetry was not for solitude,
   There seems as 'twere a curse upon the seats
   Of former sovereigns, and the antique brood
   Of Este, which for many an age made good
   Its strength within thy walls, and was of yore
   Patron or tyrant, as the changing mood
   Of petty power impelled, of those who wore
   The wreath which *Dante's* brow alone had worn before.
                            Byron.

7. And *Tasso* is their glory and their shame.
   Hark to his strain! and then survey his cell!
   And see how dearly earned Torquato's fame,
   And where Alfonso bade his poet dwell:
   The miserable despot could not quell
   The insulted mind he sought to quench, and blend
   With the surrounding maniacs, in the hell
   Where he had plunged it.   Glory without end
   Scattered the clouds away—and on that name attend.
                            Byron.

8. The lightning rent from *Ariosto's* bust
   The iron crown of laurel's mimicked leaves;
   Nor was the ominous element unjust,
   For the true laurel-wreath which glory weaves
   Is of the tree no bolt of thunder cleaves,
   And the false semblance but disgraced his brow;
   Yet still, if fondly superstition grieves,
   Know that the lightning sanctifies below
   Whate'er it strikes;—yon head is doubly sacred now.
                            Byron.

9. Ungrateful Florence!   Dante sleeps afar,
    Like Scipio, buried by the upbraiding shore;
    Thy factions, in their worse than civil war,
    Proscribed the bard whose name for evermore
    Their children's children would in vain adore
    With the remorse of ages; and the crown
    Which *Petrarch's* laureate brow supremely wore,
    Upon a far and foreign soil had grown,
    His life, his fame, his grave, though rifled—not thine
        own.
                                        Byron.

10. No matter—when some bard, in virtue strong,
    Gifford perchance, shall raise the chastening song,
    Then sleep my pen for ever! and my voice
    Be only heard to hail him and rejoice;
    Rejoice, and yield my feeble praise; though I
    May feel the lash that virtue must apply.
                                        Byron.

11. And thou, melodious *Rogers!* rise at last,
    Recall the pleasing memory of the past;
    Arise! let blest remembrance still inspire,
    And strike to wonted tones thy hallowed lyre!
    Restore Apollo to his vacant throne,
    Assert thy country's honour and thine own.
                                        Byron.

12. What! must deserted Poesy still weep
    Where her last hopes with pious *Cowper* sleep?
    Unless, perchance, from his cold bier she turns,
    To deck the turf that wraps her minstrel *Burns!*
                                        Byron.

13. Time was, ere yet in these degenerate days
    Ignoble themes obtained mistaken praise,
    When Sense and Wit with poesy allied,
    No fabled Graces, flourished side by side,
    From the same fount their inspiration drew,
    And, reared by Taste, bloomed fairer as they
        grew.
    Then, in this happy isle, a *Pope's* pure strain
    Sought the rapt soul to charm, nor sought in vain;
    A polished nation's praise aspired to claim,
    And raised the people's, as the poet's fame.

                                        Byron.

14. Unhappy *White!* while life was in its spring,
    And thy young muse just waved her joyous wing,
    The spoiler came, and all thy promise fair
    Has sought the grave, to sleep for ever there.
    Oh! what a noble heart was here undone,
    When Science' self destroyed her favourite son!
    Yes! she too much indulged thy fond pursuit,
    She sowed the seeds, but death has reaped the fruit.
    'Twas thine own genius gave the final blow,
    And helped to plant the wound that laid thee low:
    So the struck eagle, stretched upon the plain,
    No more through rolling clouds to soar again,
    Viewed his own feather on the fatal dart,
    And winged the shaft that quivered in his heart:
    Keen were his pangs, but keener far to feel
    He nursed the pinion which impelled the steel,
    While the same plumage that had warmed his nest
    Drank the last life-drop of his bleeding breast.

                                        Byron.

15. To the famed throng now paid the tribute due,
    Neglected Genius! let me turn to you.
    Come forth, O *Campbell!* give thy talents scope,
    Who dares aspire if thou must cease to hope?
                                      Byron.

16. Or, if aught in my bosom can quench for an hour
        My contempt for a nation so servile, though sore,
    Which though trod like the worm will not turn
            upon power,
        'Tis the glory of Grattan, and genius of *Moore.*
                                      Byron.

17. Say—shall this new, nor less aspiring pile,
    Reared where once rose the mightiest in our isle,
    Know the same favour which the former knew,
    A shrine for *Shakspeare*—worthy him and *you?*
                                      Byron.

18. Some persons think that *Coleridge* hath the sway;
    And Wordsworth has supporters, two or three;
    And that deep-mouthed Bœotian "Savage Landor,"
    Has taken for a swan rogue Southey's gander.
                                      Byron.

19. *John Keats*—who was killed off by one critique,
        Just as he really promised something great,
    If not intelligible, without Greek
        Contrived to talk about the gods of late,
    Much as they might have been supposed to speak.
        Poor fellow! his was an untoward fate:
    'Tis strange the mind, that very fiery particle,
    Should let itself be snuffed out by an article.
                                      Byron.

20. *Montgomery!* true, the common lot
    Of mortals lies in Lethe's wave;
    Yet some shall never be forgot—
    Some shall exist beyond the grave.

                    Byron.

21. Oh! who, that has ever had rapture complete,
    Would ask how we feel it, or why it is sweet;
    How rays are confused, or how particles fly
    Through the medium refined of a glance or a sigh!
    Is there one, who but once would not rather have
        known it,
    Than written, with *Harvey,* whole volumes upon it?

                    Moore.

22. Where *Epicurus* taught the Loves
    To polish virtue's native brightness,
    Just as the beak of playful doves
    Can give to pearls a smoother whiteness!

                    Moore.

23. Well—peace to thy heart, though another's it be,
    And health to thy cheek, though it bloom not for me!
    To-morrow, I sail for those cinnamon groves,
    Where nightly the ghost of the Carribee roves,
    And, far from thine eye, oh! perhaps, I may yet
    Its seduction forgive and its splendour forget!
    Farewell to Bermuda, and long may the bloom
    Of the lemon and myrtle its valleys perfume;
    May spring to eternity hallow the shade
    Where Ariel has warbled and *Waller* has strayed!

                    Moore.

16

24. Believe me, *Spenser*, while I winged the hours
Where Schuylkill undulates through banks of
flowers,
Though few the days, the happy evenings few,
So warm with heart, so rich with mind they flew,
That my full soul forgot its wish to roam,
And rested there, as in a dream of home!
And looks I met, like looks I loved before,
And voices too, which, as they trembled o'er
The chord of memory, found full many a tone
Of kindness there in concord with their own!
Oh! we had nights of that communion free,
That flush of heart, which I have known with thee
So oft, so warmly; nights of mirth and mind,
Of whims that taught, and follies that refined:
When shall we both renew them? when restored
To the pure feast and intellectual board,
Shall I once more enjoy with thee and thine
Those whims that teach, those follies that refine?
Even now, as wandering upon Erie's shore,
I hear Niagara's distant cataract roar,
I sigh for England—oh! these weary feet
Have many a mile to journey, ere we meet!
Moore.

25.   By Ilissus' stream
We whispering walked along, and learned
speak
The tenderest feelings in the purest Greek;
Ah! then how little did we think or hope,
Dearest of men! that I should e'er be *Pope!*
Moore.

26. My heart was full of Fancy's dream,
    And, as I watched the playful stream,
    Entangling in its net of smiles
    So fair a group of elfin isles,
    I felt as if the scenery there
        Were lighted by a Grecian sky—
    As if I breathed the blissful air
        That yet was warm with *Sappho's* sigh!
                                Moore.

27. Should you feel any touch of *poetical* glow,
    We've a scheme to suggest—Mr. *Scott*, you must
            know,
    (Who, we're sorry to say it, now works for *the Row*,)
    Having quitted the borders to seek new renown,
    Is coming, by long quarto stages, to town,
    And beginning with Rokeby (the job's sure to pay)
    Means to do all the gentlemen's seats on the way.
    Now the scheme is (though none of our hackneys
            can beat him)
    To start a fresh poet through Highgate to *meet* him;
    Who, by means of quick proofs—no revises—long
            coaches—
    May do a few Villas before Scott approaches—
    Indeed, if our Pegasus be not curst shabby,
    He'll reach, without foundering, at least Woburn-
            Abbey.
                                Moore.

28. *Herodotus* wrote most in bed;
    And Richerand, a French physician,
    Declares the clock-work of the head
        Goes best in that reclined position.
                                Moore.

29. Dear Doll, while the tails of our horses are plaiting,
    The trunks tying on, and papa at the door,
Into very bad French is, as usual, translating
    His English resolve not to give a *sou* more,
I sit down to write you a line—only think!—
A letter from France, with French pens and French
    ink,
How delightful! though, would you believe it, my
    dear?
I have seen nothing yet *very* wonderful here;
No adventure, no sentiment, far as we've come,
But the corn-fields and trees quite as dull as at
    home;
And, *but* for the post-boy, his boots, and his queue,
I might *just* as well be at Clonskilty with you!
In vain, at Dessein's, did I take from my trunk
That divine fellow, *Sterne*, and fall reading "The
    Monk!"
In vain did I think of his charming dead ass,
And remember the crust and the wallet—alas!
No monks can be had now for love or for money,
(All owing, pa says, to that infidel Boney;)
And, though *one* little Neddy we saw in our drive
Out of classical Nampont, the beast was alive!
                        Moore.

30. Your lordship beats Tiberius hollow;
    Whips, chains,—but these are things too serious
        For to me to mention or discuss;
    Whene'er your lordship acts Tiberius,
        Phil. Fudge's part is *Tacitus!*
                        Moore.

31. If you consult *Montaigne* and Pliny on
The subject, 'tis their joint opinion
That Thought its richest harvest yields
Abroad, among the woods and fields;
That bards, who deal in small retail,
    At home may, at their counters, stop:
But that the grove, the hill, the vale,
    Are Poesy's true wholesale shop.
                      Moore.

32. If thus I've felt, how must *they* feel,
    The few, whom genuine genius warms,
And stamps upon their soul his seal,
    Graven with beauty's countless forms;—
The few upon this earth who seem
Born to give truth to *Plato's* dream,
Since in their souls, as in a glass,
    Shadows of things divine appear—
Reflections of bright forms that pass
    Through fairer worlds beyond our sphere!
                      Moore.

33. But *Luther's* light had too much warmed mankind
For *Hampden's* truths to linger long behind;
Nor then, when king-like popes had fallen so low,
Could pope-like kings escape the levelling blow.
That ponderous sceptre, (in whose place we bow
To the light talisman of influence now,)
Too gross, too visible to work the spell
Which modern power performs, in fragments fell:
In fragments lay, till, patched and painted o'er
With fleurs-de-lys, it shone and scourged once more!
                      Moore.

34. Sir Robert Filmer says—and he,
    Of course, knew all about the matter—
"Both men and beasts love monarchy;"
    Which proves how rational—the latter.
Sidney, indeed, we know, had quite
A different notion from the knight;
Nay, hints a king may lose his head
    By slipping awkwardly his bridle:
But this is Jacobin, ill-bred,
And (now-a-days, when kings are led
    In patient snaffles) downright idle.

Moore.

35. Thus did *Soame Jenyns*—though a Tory,
    A lord of trade and the plantations—
Feel how religion's simple glory
    Is stained by state associations.

Moore.

36. That in this hour, when patriot zeal should guide,
    When mind should rule, and—*Fox* should *not* have
        died.

Moore.

37. "List not to reason," Epicurus cries,
    "But trust the senses, *there* conviction lies:"
Alas! *they* judge not by a purer light,
Nor keep their fountains more untinged and bright:
Habit so mars them, that the Russian swain
Will sigh for train-oil while he sips champagne;
And health so rules them, that a fever's heat
Would make even *Sheridan* think water sweet!

Moore.

38. By Tory *Hume's* seductive page beguiled,
We fancy Charles was just and Strafford mild;
And Fox himself, with party pencil, draws
Monmouth a hero, "for the good old cause!"
Then, rights are wrongs, and victories are defeats,
As French or English pride the tale repeats;
And, when they tell Corunna's story o'er,
They'll disagree in all, but honouring Moore!
Moore.

39. In science too—how many a system, raised
Like Neva's icy domes, awhile hath blazed
With lights of fancy and with forms of pride,
Then, melting, mingled with the oblivious tide.
Now earth usurps the centre of the sky,
Now Newton puts the paltry planet by;
Now whims revive beneath Descartes's pen,
Which *now*, assailed by *Locke's*, expire again:
And when, perhaps, in pride of chemic powers,
We think the keys of Nature's kingdom ours,
Some Davy's magic touch the dream unsettles,
And turns at once our alkalis to metals!
Moore.

40. Give me the harp of epic song,
Which *Homer's* finger thrilled along;
But tear away the sanguine string,
For war is not the theme I sing.
Proclaim the laws of festal rite,
I'm monarch of the board to-night;
And all around shall brim as high,
And quaff the tide as deep as I!
Moore.

41. O Learning! Learning! whatsoe'er thy boast,
    Unlettered minds have taught and charmed us most:
    The rude, unread Columbus was our guide
    To worlds which learned Lactantius had denied,
    And one wild *Shakspeare*, following Nature's lights,
    Is worth whole planets filled with Stagyrites!
                            Moore.

42. Oh thou! whatever title please thine ear—
    Dean, Drapier, Bickerstaff, or Gulliver!
    Whether thou choose Cervantes' serious air,
    Or laugh and shake in Rabelais' easy chair,
    Or praise the court, or magnify mankind,
    Or thy grieved country's copper chains unbind,
    From thy Bœotia though her power retires,
    Mourn not, my *Swift*, at aught our realm acquires.
    Here pleased behold her mighty wings outspread
    To hatch a new Saturnian age of lead.
                            Pope.

43. Next o'er his books his eyes began to roll,
    In pleasing memory of all he stole,
    How here he sipped, how here he plundered snug,
    And sucked all o'er like an industrious bug.
    Here lay poor *Fletcher's* half-eat scenes, and here
    The frippery of crucified Molière:
    There hapless Shakspeare, yet of Tibbald sore,
    Wished he had blotted for himself before.
                            Pope.

44. Be thine, my stationer! this magic gift;
    Cook shall be *Prior:* and Concanen, Swift.
                            Pope.

45. Small thanks to France, and none to Rome or Greece,
   A past, vamped, future, old, revived, new piece,
   'Twixt Plautus, Fletcher, Shakspeare, and *Corqeille*,
   Can make a Cibber, Tibbald, or Ozell.

   Pope.

46. So shall each hostile name become our own,
   And we too boast our Garth and *Addison*.

   Pope.

47. Earless on high, stood unabashed *De Foe*,
   And Tutchin flagrant from the scourge below.

   Pope.

48. Yet oh, my sons, a father's words attend:
   (So may the fates preserve the ears you lend:)
   'Tis yours, a Bacon or a Locke to blame,
   A Newton's genius, or a Milton's flame:
   But oh! with One, immortal One dispense,
   The source of Newton's light, of *Bacon's* sense.

   Pope.

49. See under Ripley rise a new Whitehall,
   While Jones' and Boyle's united labours fall;
   While Wren with sorrow to the grave descends,
   Gay dies unpensioned, with a hundred friends;
   Hibernian politics, O Swift! thy fate;
   And Pope's, ten years to comment and translate.

   Pope.

50. There sunk Thalia, nerveless, cold, and dead,
   Had not her sister Satire held her head:
   Nor couldst thou, *Chesterfield!* a tear refuse!
   Thou wept'st, and with thee wept each gentle muse.

   Pope.

Which is your Favourite Bird?

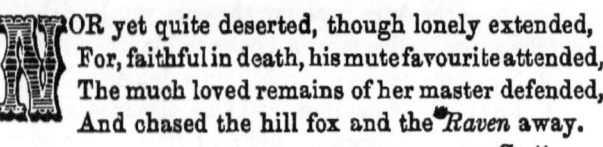OR yet quite deserted, though lonely extended,
For, faithful in death, his mute favourite attended,
The much loved remains of her master defended,
And chased the hill fox and the *Raven* away.

Scott.

2. 'Twas a fair scene! the sunbeam lay
   On battled tower and portal gray,
   And from the grassy slope he sees
   The Greta flow to meet the Tees,
   Where, issuing from her darksome bed,
   She caught the morning's eastern red,
   And through the softening vale below
   Rolled her bright waves in rosy glow,
   All blushing to her bridal bed,
   Like some shy maid in convent bred,
   While linnet, lark, and *Blackbird* gay,
   Sing forth her nuptial roundelay.

Scott.

3. But meeter for thee, gentle lover of nature,
    To lay down thy head like the meek mountain lamb;
  When, wildered, he drops from some cliff huge in
      stature,
    And draws his last sob by the side of his dam.
    And more stately thy couch by this desert lake lying
    Thy obsequies sung by the *Gray Plover* flying,
    With one faithful friend but to witness thy dying,
    In the arms of Hellvellyn and Catchedicam.
                              Scott.

4. The *Bittern* clamoured from the moss,
    The wind blew loud and shrill;
  Yet the craggy pathway she did cross,
    To the eiry beacon hill.
                              Scott.

5. As from the bosom of the sky
    The *Eagle* darts amain,
  Three bounds from yonder summit high
    Placed Harold on the plain.
                              Scott.

6. As the scared wild-fowl scream and fly,
    So fled the bridal train;
  As 'gainst the eagle's peerless might
  The noble *Falcon* dares the fight,
    But dares the fight in vain,
  So fought the bridegroom; from his hand
  The Dane's rude mace has struck his brand,
  Its glittering fragments strew the sand,
    Its lord lies on the plain.
                              Scott.

7. Each bird of evil omen woke,
   The raven gave his fatal croak,
   And shrieked the night-crow from the oak,
   The *Screech-owl* from the thicket broke,
     And fluttered down the dell!
   So fearful was the sound and stern,
   The slumbers of the full-gorged erne
   Were startled, and from furze and fern,
     Of forest and of fell,
   The fox and famished wolf replied,
   (For wolves then prowled the Cheviot side,)
   From mountain head to mountain head
   The unhallowed sounds around were sped;
   But when their latest echo fled,
   The sorceress on the ground lay dead.

Scott.

8. The hunting tribes of air and earth
   Respect the brethren of their birth;
   Nature, who loves the claim of kind,
   Less cruel chase to each assigned.
   The falcon poised on soaring wing,
   Watches the *Wild-duck* by the spring;
   The slow-hound wakes the fox's lair,
   The grey-hound presses on the hare;
   The eagle pounces on the lamb,
   The wolf devours the fleecy dam;
   E'en tiger fell, and sullen bear,
   Their likeness and their lineage spare.
   Man, only, mars kind nature's plan,
   And turns the fierce pursuit on man.

Scott.

9. Hoarse into middle air arose
   The vesper of the roosting *Crows*,
   And with congenial murmurs seem
   To wake the genii of the stream.

                                        Scott.

10. Autumn departs—but still his mantle's fold
      Rests on the groves of noble Somerville,
    Beneath a shroud of russet dropped with gold,
      Tweed and his tributaries mingle still;
    Hoarser the wind, and deeper sounds the rill
      Yet lingering notes of sylvan music swell,
    The deep-toned *Cushat*, and the redbreast shrill;
      And yet some tints of summer splendour tell
    When the broad sun sinks down on Ettrick's west-
      ern fell.

                                        Scott.

11. The shores of Mull on the eastward lay,
    And Ulva dark and Colonsay,
    And all the group of islets gay
      That guard famed Staffa round.
    Then all unknown its columns rose,
    Where dark and undisturbed repose
      The *Cormorant* had found,
    And the shy seal had quiet home,
    And weltered in that wonderous dome,
    Where, as to shame the temples decked
    By skill of earthly architect,
    Nature herself, it seemed, would raise
    A minster to her Maker's praise!

                                        Scott

12. See, sister, where the *Chickens* trip,
       All busy in the morn;
   Look! how their heads they dip and dip,
       To peck the scattered corn.
   Dear sister, shall we shut our eyes,
       And to the sight be blind,
   Nor think of Him who food supplies
       To us and all mankind!
   Whether our wants be much or few,
       Or fine or coarse our fare,
   To Heaven's protecting care is due
       The voice of praise and prayer.
                                 Bowles.

13. Merrily, merrily, goes the bark
       On a breeze from the northward free,
   So shoots through the morning sky the lark,
       Or the *Swan* through the summer sea.
                                 Scott.

14. The bee is humming in the sun,
       The yellow cowslip springs,
   And hark! from yonder woodland's side
       Again the *Cuckoo* sings!
   Cuckoo—Cuckoo! no other note,
       She sings from day to day;
   But I, though a poor cottage-girl,
       Can work, and read, and pray.
   And whilst in knowledge I rejoice,
       Which heavenly truth displays,
   Oh! let me still employ my voice
       In my Redeemer's praise.
                                 Bowles.

15. The bow is gone, the *Hawk* is thrown
     For ever from the hand;
   And now we live a bookish race,
     All in a cultured land.

                                   Howitt.

16. Poor *Robin* sits and sings alone,
     When showers of driving sleet,
   By the cold winds of winter blown,
     The cottage casement beat.
   Come, let him share our chimney-nook,
     And dry his dripping wing;
   See, little Mary shuts her book,
     And cries, "Poor Robin, sing."
   Methinks I hear his faint reply—
     When cowslips deck the plain,
   The lark shall carol in the sky,
     And I shall sing again.
   But in the cold and wintry day
     To you I owe a debt,
   That in the sunshine of the May
     I never can forget.

                                   Bowles.

17. O stormy, *Stormy Peterel*,
     Come rest thee, bird, awhile;
   There is no storm, believe me,
     Anigh this summer isle.
   Come, rest thy waving pinions;
     Alight thee down by me;
   And tell me somewhat of the lore
     Thou learnest on the sea!

Dost hear beneath the ocean
   The gathering tempest form?
See'st thou afar the little cloud
   That grows into the storm?
How is it in the billowy depths—
   Doth sea-weed heave and swell?
And is a sound of coming wo
   Rung from each caverned shell?
Dost watch the stormy sunset
   In tempests of the west;
And see the old moon riding slow
   With the new moon on her breast?

                           Howitt.

18. Fern-owl, churn-owl, or goat-sucker,
     Night-jar, dor-hawk, or whate'er
  Be thy name among a dozen,—
  Whip-poor-will's and who-are-you's cousin,
  Chuck-will's-widow's near relation,
  Thou art at thy night vocation,
     Thrilling the still evening air!
  In the dark brown wood beyond us,
     Where the night lies·dusk and deep;
  Where the fox his furrow maketh,
  Where the tawny owl awaketh
     Nightly from his day-long sleep;
  There, *Dor-hawk*, is thy abiding,
     Meadow green is not for thee;
  While the aspen branches shiver,
  Mid the roaring of the river,
     Comes thy chirring voice to me.

                           Howitt.

19. Not down the breeze more blithely flew,
    Skimming the wave, the light *Sea-mew*,
    Than the gay galley bore
    Her course upon that favouring wind,
    And Coolin's crest has sunk behind,
    And Slapin's caverned shore.

    Scott.

20. The *Curlew* and the plover,
    The gor-cock on the brae,
    Send, with the singing of the lark,
    Their voices far away!

    Howitt.

21. The coot and *Moor-hen* from the reeds,
    Or where the waters run
    Crystal and warm and glittering,
    O'er the pebbles in the sun.

    Howitt.

22. Of the big-bone lick, did you say?—Ay, we used to
    go there.
    A *Parrot's* very fond of salt! I really declare
    I've seen ten thousand of us there altogether.—
    A beautiful sight it was, in fine summer weather,
    Like a grand velvet carpet, of orange, green, and
    yellow,
    Covering the ground! Ah, Captain! my good fellow,
    I had reason to rue the day you came there with
    your gun!
    I would laugh if I could, but to me it was no fun—
    heigh-ho!
    No fun at all, Captain, heigh-ho!

    Howitt.

17

23. Lo! there the hermit of the waste,
     The ghost of ages dim,
The fisher of the solitudes,
     Stands by the river's brim!
Old *Heron*, in the feudal times,
     Beside the forest stream,
And by the moorland waters,
     Thus didst thou love to dream.
And over towers and castles high,
     And o'er the armed men,
Skirmishing on the border-lands,
     Or crouching in the glen;
Thy heavy wings were seen to flit,
     Thy azure shape was known
To pilgrim and to anchorite,
     In deserts scorched and lone.

                                        Howitt.

24. The stockdove builds in the old oak wood,
     The *Rook* in the elm-tree rears his brood;
     The owl in a ruin doth hoot and stare;
     The mavis and merle build everywhere.

                                        Howitt.

25. Away to the woods with the silvery rind,
     And the emerald tresses afloat on the wind!
     For 'tis joy to go to those sylvan bowers
     When summer is rich with leaves and flowers;
     And to see, mid the growth of all lovely things,
     The joyous *Pheasant* unfold his wings,
     And then cower down, as if to screen
     His gorgeous purple, gold, and green!

                                        Howitt.

26. *Raven*, on the blasted tree,
    Sitting croaking dolefully,
    I would have a word with thee!
    Raven, thou art silent now
    On the splintered forest bough,
    Glancing on me thy bright eye,
    I shall ask,—do thou reply!
    In that far-gone, awful time,
    When the earth was purged of crime,
    And old Noah and the seven
    In the gopher-ark were driven.
              Howitt.

27. Speed messengers the country through;
    Arouse old friends, and gather new;
    Warn Lanark's knights to gird their mail,
    Rouse the brave sons of Teviotdale,
    Let Ettrick's archers sharp their darts,
    The fairest forms, the truest hearts!
    Call all, call all! from Reedswair path,
    To the wild confines of Cape-Wrath;
    Wide let the news through Scotland ring,
    The *Northern Eagle* claps his wing!
              Scott.

28. The *Stock-doves* together begin to coo
    When they hear the voice of the old cuckoo;
    "Ho! ho!" say they, "he did not find
    Those far-away countries quite to his mind,
    So he's come again to see what he can do
    With sucking the small birds' eggs, coo-coo!"
              Howitt.

29. At once ten thousand bow-strings ring,
    Ten thousand arrows fly!
Nor paused on the devoted Scot
The ceaseless fury of their shot;
    As fiercely and as fast,
Forth whistling came the *Gray-goose* wing,
As the wild hail-stones pelt and ring
Adown December's blast.

                          Scott.

30 Hawk and *Osprey* screamed for joy,
O'er the beetling cliffs of Hoy,
Crimson foam the beach o'erspread,
The heath was dyed with darker red,
When o'er Erick, Inguar's son,
Dane and Northman piled the stone;
Singing wild the war-song stern,
Rest thee, Dweller of the Cairn!

                          Scott.

31. The *Woodpecker* laughs to hear the strain,
And says "The old fellow is come back again;
He sitteth again on the very same tree,
And he talks of himself again!—he! he! he!"

                          Howitt.

32. In town or country—in the densest alley
Of monstrous London—in the loneliest valley—
On palace-roof—on cottage-thatch,
On church or chapel—farm or shop,
The *Sparrow*'s still "the bird on the house-top."

                          Howitt.

33. The *Black-bird*, and throstle, and loud missel-cock,
They sing altogether, the Cuckoo to mock;
"What want we with him? let him stay over sea!"
Sings the bold, piping reed-sparrow, "Want him?
     not we!"
"Cuckoo!" the Cuckoo shouts still,
"I care not for you, let you rave as you will!"
"Cuckoo!" the Cuckoo doth cry,
And the little boys mock him as they go by.
                                        Howitt.

34. O gay *Goshawk* and tercel bold,
Then might ye rule it as ye "wold;"
Then sate ye on a perch of gold,
     And kings were your compeers!
But that was in the days gone by;
The days of Norman chivalry,
When the low crouched unto the high;—
     The times of other years!
                                        Howitt.

35. There the hum of the bees through the noonday is
          heard,
And the chirp, and the cry, and the song of the bird;
There up the tree-trunk, like a fly on the wall,
To pick the gray moss, runs the tree-creeper small;
There the wren golden-crested, so lovely to see,
Hangs its delicate nest from the twigs of the tree;
And there coos the *Ring-dove*—oh, who would not go,
That voice of the wood to hear, dreamy and low!
Yes, come to the wood—to the woodpecker's tree,
There is joy 'mong the green leaves for thee and for
          me!
                                        Howitt.

36. The merry *Titmouse* is a comical fellow;
      He weareth a plumage of purple and yellow,
      Barred over with black, and with white interlaced;—
      Depend on't, the titmouse has excellent taste.
      And he, like his betters of noble old blood,
      Keeps up, with great spirit, a family feud.;
      A feud with the owl;—and why? would you know;—
      An old, bygone quarrel of ages ago:—
      Perhaps in the ark might be taken offence,—
      But I know not, indeed, of the where and the
           whence;—
      Only this is quite true,—let them meet as they may,
      Having quarrelled long since, they would quarrel
           to-day.

                               Howitt.

37. O lovely *Bird of Paradise*,
      I'll go where thou dost go!
      Rise higher yet, and higher yet,
      For a stormy wind doth blow.
      Now up above the tempest
      We are sailing in the calm,
      Amid the golden sunshine,
      And where the air is balm.
      See, far below us rolling,
      The storm-cloud black and wide;
      The fury of its raging
      Is as an angry tide!
      O gentle bird of paradise,
      Thy happy lot I'll share;
      And go where'er thou goest
      On, through the sunny air!

                               Howitt.

38 O *Falcon* proud, and goshawk gay,
   Your pride of place has passed away;
   The lone wood is your home by day,
     Your resting perch by night;
   The craggy rock your castle-tower;
   The gay green-wood your ladies' bower;
   Your own wild will, the master power
     That can control your flight!
Howitt.

39. Pray thee, *Owl*, what art thou doing,
   With that dolefulest tu-whoo-ing?
   Dark the night is, dark and dreary,
   Never a little star shines cheery;
   Wild north winds come up the hollow,
   And the pelting rain doth follow;
   And the trees, the tempest braving,
   To and fro are wildly waving!
   Every living thing is creeping
   To its den, and silence keeping,
   Saving thou, the night hallooing
   With thy dismalest tu-whooing!
Howitt.

40. Then softly, softly will we tread
     By inland streams, to see
   Where the *Pelican* of the silent north,
     Sits there all silently.
   But if thou love the Southern Seas,
     And pleasant summer weather,
   Come, let us mount this gallant ship,
     And sail away together.
Howitt.

41. The *Woodpecker* green he has not his abiding
   Where the owls and the bats from the daylight are
        hiding;
   Where the bright mountain-streams glide on rock-
        beds away,
   The dark water-ousel may warble and play;
   In the sedge of the river the reed-sparrow build;
   And the peewit among the brown clods of the field;
   The sea-gull may scream on the breast of the tide;
   On the foam-crested billows the peterel may ride;
   But the woodpecker asketh nor river nor sea;
   Give him but the old forest, and old forest-tree,
   And he'll leave to the proud lonely eagle the height
   Of the mist-shrouded precipice splintered and white;
   And he'll leave to the gorcock the heather and fern,
   And the lake of the valley to woodcock and hern;
   To the skylark he'll leave the wild fields of the air,
   The sunshine and rainbow ne'er tempted him there;
   The greenwood for him is the place of his rest,
   And the broad-branching tree is the home he loves
        best.
   Let us go to the haunt of the woodpecker green,
   In those depths of the wood there is much to be
        seen.

Howitt.

42. Not in the land of a thousand flowers,
   Not in the glorious spice-wood bowers;
   Not in fair islands by bright seas embraced,
   Lives the wild *Ostrich*, the bird of the waste.
   Come on to the desert, his dwelling is there,
   Where the breath of the Simoom is hot in the air;

To the desert, where never a green blade grew,
Where never its shadow a broad tree threw,
Where sands rise up, and in columns are wheeled
By the winds of the desert, like hosts in the field;
Where the wild ass sends forth a lone, dissonant
  bray,
And the herds of the wild horse speed on through
  the day—
The creatures unbroken, with manes flying free,
Like the steeds of the whirlwind, if such there may
  be.
Yes, there in the desert, like armies for war,
The flocks of the *ostrich* are seen from afar,
Speeding on, speeding on o'er the desolate plain,
While the fleet mounted Arab pursueth in vain!
But 'tis joy to the traveller who toils through that
  land,
The egg of the ostrich to find in the sand;
'Tis sustenance for him when his store is low,
And weary with travel he journeyeth slow
To the well of the desert, and finds it at last
Seven days' journey from that he hath passed.

Howitt.

43. In books of travels I have heard
    Of a wise thing, the *Tailor-bird;*
    A bird of wondrous skill, that sews,
    Upon the bough whereon it grows,
    A leaf into a nest so fair
    That with it nothing can compare;
    A light and lovely airy thing,
    That vibrates with the breeze's wing.

Ah well! it is with cunning power
That little artist makes her bower;
But come into an English wood,
And I'll show you a work as good,
A work the tailor-bird's excelling,
A more elaborate, snugger dwelling,
More beautiful, upon my word,
Wrought by a little English bird.

Howitt.

44. No, not in the meadow, and not on the shore;
And not on the wide heath with furze covered o'er,
Where the cry of the plover, the hum of the bee,
Give a feeling of joyful security:
And not in the woods, where the *Nightingale's* song
From the chestnut and orange pours all the day long,
And not where the martin has built in the eaves,
And the redbreast e'er covered the children with
    leaves,
Shall ye find the proud eagle! O no, come away;
I will show you his dwelling, and point out his prey.

Howitt.

45. For the handsome *Kingfisher*, go not to the tree,
No bird of the field or the forest is he;
In the dry riven rock he did never abide,
And not on the brown heath all barren and wide.
He lives where the fresh, sparkling waters are
    flowing,
Where the tall, heavy Typha and Loosestrife are
    growing;
By the bright little streams that all joyfully run
Awhile in the shadow, and then in the sun.

He lives in a hole that is quite to his mind,
With the green, mossy hazel roots firmly entwined;
Where the dark alder-bough waves gracefully o'er,
And the sword-flag and arrow-head grow at his door.
There busily, busily, all the day long,
He seeks for small fishes the shallows among;
For he builds his nest of the pearly fish-bone,
Deep, deep in the bank far retired, and alone.
Then the brown water-rat from his burrow looks
        out,
To see what his neighbour kingfisher's about;
And the green dragon-fly, flitting slowly away,
Just pauses one moment to bid him good-day,
O happy kingfisher! what care should he know,
By the clear, pleasant streams, as he skims to and
        fro,
Now lost in the shadow, now bright in the sheen
Of the hot summer sun, glancing scarlet and green!
                                        Howitt.

46. The *Humming-bird!* the humming-bird,
        So fairy-like and bright;
    It lives among the sunny flowers,
        A creature of delight!
    In the radiant islands of the East,
        Where fragrant spices grow,
    A thousand thousand humming-birds
        Go glancing to and fro.
    Like living fires they flit about,
        Scarce larger than a bee,
    Among the broad palmetto leaves,
        And through the fan-palm tree.

And in those wild and verdant woods
  Where stately moras tower,
Where hangs from branching tree to tree
  The scarlet passion-flower;
Where on the mighty river banks,
  La Platte or Amazon,
The cayman, like an old tree trunk,
  Lies basking in the sun;
There builds her nest the humming-bird
  Within the ancient wood,
Her nest of silky cotton down,
  And rears her tiny brood.
She hangs it to a slender twig,
  Where waves it light and free,
As the Campanero tolls his song,
  And rocks the mighty tree.

                       Howitt.

47. All crimson is her shining breast,
   Like to the red, red rose;
  Her wing is the changeful green and blue
   That the neck of the *Peacock* shows.

                       Howitt.

48. *Swan* of the ocean, on thy throne of waves
  Exultant dost thou sit, thy mantling plumes
  Ruffled with joy, thy pride of neck elate,
  To hail fair peace, like angel visitant,
  Descending amid joy of earth and heaven,
  To bless thy fair abode.

                       Milman.

49. Twittering *Swallow*, fluttering swallow,
    Art come back again?
Come from water-bed or hollow,
    Where thou, winter-long, hast lain?
Nay, I'll not believe it, swallow,
Not in England hast thou tarried;
        Many a day
        Far away
Has thy wing been wearied,
Over continent and isle,
Many and many and many a mile!
Tell me, pr'ythee bird, the story
Of thy six months migratory!
If thou wert a human traveller,
    We a quarto book should see;
Thou wouldst be the sage unraveller
    Of some dark old mystery;
Thou wouldst tell the wise men, swallow,
Of the rivers' hidden fountains;
        Plain and glen,
        And savage men,
And Afghauns of the mountains;
Creatures, plants, and men unknown,
And cities in the deserts lone:
Thou wouldst be, thou far-land dweller,
Like an Arab story-teller!

                       Howitt

50. *Dove* of the wilderness, thy snowy wing
    In slumber droops not; Lilian, thou alone,
    Mid the deep quiet, wakest. Dost thou rove,
    Idolatrous of yon majestic moon,

That like a crystal-throned queen in heaven,
Seems with her present deity to hush
To beauteous adoration all the earth?
Might seem the solemn silent mountain tops
Stand up and worship, the translucent streams
Down the hill sides glittering cherish the pure light
Beneath the shadowy foliage o'er them flung
At intervals; the lake, so silver white,
Glistens, all indistinct the snowy swans
Bask in the radiance cool; doth Lilian muse
To that apparent queen her vesper hymn?

Milman.

THE END.

www.ingramcontent.com/pod-product-compliance
Lightning Source LLC
Chambersburg PA
CBHW030634030726
47497CB00006B/1782